"Davis presents an evangelical ur
cate interplay of eternal design and cultural choices in an errort to can
the church back to a biblical understanding of her design and purpose." —*David Maltsberger, Ph.D., Assistant professor of Biblical Studies at Baptist University of the Americas*

"In his new book, *Culture Wars*, Dr. Freddy Davis has laid out for us several of the main worldviews in the contemporary context we find ourselves in. He has attempted to equip us with the tools to choose and understand our own worldview...and to defend it. The real skill is found in how accessible he has made some very difficult material. He has written to 'Everyman' and has the means to communicate this very important material in a way that makes this book an important book for any Christian to read."
—*D.E. "Gene" Mills, Jr., Senior Assistant to the editors of* Church History: Studies in Christianity and Culture *magazine* -

"Dealing with individuals shaped by a culture that is not our own is fast becoming every person's challenge. Christians, in particular, should see this is an opportunity. Freddy Davis provides us that opportunity in his book, *Culture Wars*."
—*J. David Southerland, Executive Director, Florida Baptist Association*

"Freddy Davis carries passion and insight into an area where many people fear to tread: worldview discussions. But he has made these drastically important discussions accessible with language and examples that the everyday person can understand. In an age where the Judeo-Christian worldview is not the standard on the street, I find that 'loving thy neighbor' is just as much about kindness as it is about shedding light. This book invites the reader into shining that light with clarity and gives suggestive reading for more in-depth study."
—*Dale Fincher, Soulation, Inc., Apologist, Writer, Storyteller, formerly on the itinerant apologetics team of Ravi Zacharias*

Culture
WARS

What You Believe
Does Matter!

Freddy Davis

E*ergreen
PRESS

ISBN 1-58169-201-3
For Worldwide Distribution
Printed in the U.S.A.

Evergreen Press
P.O. Box 191540 • Mobile, AL 36619
800-367-8203

Table of Contents

Preface

My purpose in this book is to try and take a very complex topic and put it in terms that we average folks can understand. As you read this, I am sure that there are some things written here that you will agree with and some you will disagree with. I respect that. In fact, given that we are all trying to make sense of a spiritual reality that we can't experience with our physical senses, it could hardly be otherwise. There are certain things we know without doubt because God considered them important enough to give us an absolutely clear revelation. There are many other things, though, that we have to try to make sense of that are not nearly so clear.

As you read, I hope you can, personally, look beyond the places where you might disagree with me and focus more on the basic concepts that underlie all of life. I want you to be able to see how grasping the notion of worldview can give you a new understanding and confidence about your own belief system and how it ought to be played out in life. In doing so, you will become more effective in carrying out the purposes of God in your life.

Acknowledgments

Of all the books I have written, this one has been the most complex and time consuming. The process of trying to take a very complex and technical topic and simplify it has been a much more daunting task than I could have ever imagined. I am deeply indebted to many people who have been gracious and kind to me above and beyond the call of duty.

I first want to thank my wife, Deborah, and my son, Ken, for allowing themselves to be a sounding board for me. Deborah read the manuscript several times and kept my feet planted firmly in reality. Ken allowed me to work through the material with him personally which allowed me to refine the things I needed to say.

I also want to thank three scholars and experts who were gracious enough to read the manuscript in its early stages and warn me of potential minefields I was about to step in. None of them are responsible in any way for any dumb stuff that might have ended up in the book, but there certainly would have been a lot more if not for them. I want to thank Dr. James Sire with InterVarsity Fellowship, Mr. Dale Fincher who was formerly with Ravi Zacharias Ministries and now has his own ministry called Soulation, and Mr. Dan Smithwick with the Nehemiah Institute.

I also want to give a huge thank-you to Heeth Varnedoe who believed in me and showed his very tangible encouragement at a time when things were a bit rough. Without his support, I don't believe this project would have happened.

There are too many others to mention individually who helped by looking over the manuscript, making suggestions and offering other kinds of help. To everyone who played any part at all in this, I owe my deepest appreciation and will not forget your belief in me.

Introduction

From 1920 to 1933, a "noble experiment" was undertaken in America to try and reduce crime and corruption, improve health, solve social problems and reduce the prison population. That experiment was called Prohibition—the elimination of the manufacture and sale of alcoholic beverages.

Personally, I agree with the goals of Prohibition—who wouldn't want to eliminate all those social evils? In that day, alcohol was identified, particularly by the Christian community, as a societal evil that ruined people's lives. As a result, movements were created and laws were passed which finally made the manufacture and sale of alcohol illegal. But the movement didn't just emerge overnight and all of a sudden there was a national law. Rather, it moved forward for literally dozens of years, community by community and state by state, until it became so strong that Congress could not keep from passing the national Prohibition laws.

By all accounts the laws were a miserable failure, and after thirteen years they were repealed. Now, as we take the lessons from this historical event and try to learn from them, we have to look at a broader set of principles. The most important issue, both in that day and in our current time, is not agreement or disagreement with a particular set of laws. (Of course, this is not to say that laws, themselves, are inconsequential. It's just that there is something more significant here than that.) The important questions relate to why a noble cultural movement was able to move forward so powerfully for so long, yet not endure. You see, alcohol was the hot button issue of the culture war back in that day. The anti-alcohol crowd were the Christians who wanted to eliminate an obvious evil from society. So why did they end up losing so badly after such great initial success?

Every once in a while we find ourselves in a situation where we are caused to think more deeply than usual about some aspect of life. Sometimes it happens when we hear a particularly stirring speech or sermon. Often it happens after some tragedy or other life altering event. There was a profound and obvious movement in this direction by all of America after the events of 9/11/2001. Other times we are caused to ponder life more deeply when an obvious evil begins to permeate society to the point that it becomes offensive beyond toleration.

As believers in Jesus Christ, when we are caused to think about the right way to live, most of us intuitively understand that living life as a committed Christian is the direction we ought to take. That concept certainly applies to our personal thoughts and actions. But it also extends out beyond our own skin and affects how our beliefs fit into the overall cultural environment we live in.

I believe that most people who love God have a deep desire to personally live a life which is in line with God's standards. On top of that, we want to live in a society which also displays those values. But the fact of the matter is, there is a huge and growing segment of the population which lives by an entirely different set of values—one that is totally contrary to Christian values.

In our day, alcohol is still somewhat in the mix of issues that are fought over in the culture war. But there are even bigger ones. We see a massive clash in values over issues such as the value of life, the proper understanding of sexuality, the definition of family, the place of religion in public life, the role of government in the private and public sectors and a host of other issues. There is an entirely different set of beliefs about life and reality which is challenging the traditional Christian understanding that American culture was founded upon.

It is at this point that we must begin to come to an understanding of the task at hand. How do we go about fighting the culture war and what can we do to make sure that the final result is different from what happened with Prohibition?

What we must understand is that the answer does not lie in our attempts to deal head on with the particular outward expressions of the culture war. Rather, it lies in our foundational understanding of the nature of our existence.

At first glance this may seem a bit philosophical and academic. But we live in a world where various ways of thinking about, and experiencing, life are in fierce conflict. People with different belief systems are giving voice to, and living out, their various "faiths" in our living space. These various beliefs are blasted from the media, pushed on us from powerful political, business, religious and cultural interests, and taught in our educational institutions. With all of the conflicting messages constantly bombarding us, it is no wonder that we live in confusion and that we struggle with how to live out a Christian worldview.

As Christians, the problem that most of us struggle with, without even realizing it, is that we really don't have a clear sense of the battle we are in. We hear the messages of humanists, secularists, naturalists, modernists, existentialists, post-modernists, new-agers, Buddhists, Hindus, Muslims, animists, and a whole host of others, and don't know how to deal with them. It is much easier to see the particular elements we disagree with in these various belief systems and simply work to eliminate these "symptoms" rather than identify the underlying beliefs and work at that level.

But the really important issues relate to those very underlying issues. We need to figure out how other ideas and values differ from Christian ones. Are they superior, inferior or the same? If we can't figure this out, there is no way for us to make clear decisions and commitments as to how we are going to live out our faith.

Unfortunately, most of us who consider ourselves Christians don't have a clear understanding of these issues. We recognize that other beliefs are different from ours, and may even recognize what many of the differences are. But we don't have compelling personal reasons to pick our Christian faith over other belief systems to the point that we feel driven to stand up and defend it. Rather, we tend to dilute our beliefs by mixing them together with others. Many people have the philosophy, "Who are we to say that our way of believing is superior to someone else's?"

Let me be right up front from the beginning. This book is based on the assumption that the worldview represented in the Bible is the truth about life. More than that, it is the only way to organize reality so that it matches up with the way the universe actually operates.

Some readers may think that this is a somewhat arrogant statement. But the fact is, you think that way, too, with your basic beliefs as your bottom line assumptions. It's just that I have dared to state specifically what my beliefs are built upon.

A very large percentage of Christians (perhaps even a majority) simply do not have the confidence to put forth their faith as the model for everyone else to follow. Sometimes it is because they don't really understand their own faith. Sometimes it is because they are not willing to be an offense to people who have other value systems. Sometimes it is because they are not willing to give up a lifestyle that is incompatible with Christian faith. There is no way to deal with all the possible belief issues in this one book. But it is important to get started.

When federal treasury agents are taught how to detect counterfeit currency, they do not study counterfeit currency—they study the real thing. Then, when they come across something that is not right, they recognize it immediately. We have to do the same thing with our faith.

The Bible teaches us that when we enter into a relationship with God we become citizens of the Kingdom of God. As with any society, there are a lot of facets to this kingdom. There is a political part, an economic part and a social part. There are laws that must be obeyed, values that must be followed, ways of thinking that must be adhered to and ways of relating to others that must be respected. In other words, there is a specific culture that can be referred to as "Kingdom culture." People who are Kingdom citizens are commanded by God to make this culture their priority—above any material culture they interact in. If we know Kingdom culture as well as treasury agents know their currency, we will not have any real difficulty moving in the right direction.

The problem we face, as we try to understand the nature of our existence, is that the Kingdom and the Kingdom culture are spiritual. While it has definite material expressions, we can't view it in quite the same way as we do material cultures. For most people, material culture seems more real and compelling. To make it even more difficult,

Kingdom culture conflicts, at certain points, with every other culture that exists on the face of the earth. That is why we have the culture war battles over issues such as marriage, sexuality, abortion and the rest. Even among Christians, the great tendency is to try to make God's Kingdom culture fit into our material lives. The problem is, this kind of thinking is completely backward. Rather, we need to be working to make our material lives fit into Kingdom culture.

There is one other facet to this culture war that creates difficulty for us. It is not enough to learn how to live our lives as Kingdom citizens in a material culture. We are also admonished to be soldiers in the army of the Kingdom in order to conquer and transform material culture to conform to the values of God's Kingdom. Don't let the military metaphor throw you off. This is not a reference to physical fighting which results in some kind of Christian "jihad." Rather, it is the process of understanding the purpose of God and our place in it, as we do the work of God to lead people into a relationship with him.

And here is where the confusion and difficulty come in. What most people try to do is identify the parts of material culture that conflict with Kingdom culture, then go out and try to change them. We create movements and try to pass laws to make that happen.

Now don't misunderstand. Sometimes it is necessary to create movements and pass laws. It is important because culture is going to be guided by one set of values or another. We certainly want a set of values in place which supports the very best aspects of human society—and that is definitely Christian values. But without another support piece, that effort is ultimately a futile exercise. Material culture does, indeed, need to be changed. But it will never be done by focusing on the culture itself. The focus has to be elsewhere.

For every element of culture there is an underlying set of ideas which are its foundation. To change a culture, it is necessary to identify the foundation and attack at that level. What this means is that we have to help the people with wrong foundations to see their errors by working with them on the level of belief. When enough people make a change at this level, outward material culture will automatically change. If we don't take this approach, we will end up with the same result that the Prohibitionists did.

This book is a journey into the means of conforming to and spreading Kingdom culture. It is an attempt to understand it, compare it with our material culture, discover ways we can conform ourselves to the culture of the Kingdom of God, and figure out how we can be effective soldiers in the culture war. Let us now begin this journey and learn how to understand and promote the Kingdom of God in the world of men.

I have found that there are two levels of understanding that we must possess in the learning process. The first is *intellectual understanding*. This is where we study something enough that we know what is going on in that area. Before we can ever use any kind of information, we have to grasp it in a way that allows us to make sense of it.

But that is not enough. I am not a mechanically inclined person so I don't try to work on cars. I do, though, sometimes watch my mechanic work and ask him questions. When I do, I basically understand what he is talking about. But that intellectual knowledge does not translate into my being able to do the work.

The second level of understanding is *experiential knowledge*. This is where we are able to take the knowledge we have and actually do something with it.

We live in a very complex world with lots of different, even conflicting, beliefs. It is one thing to know what is true. It is something else all together to make sense of it and use that knowledge effectively in life's relationships.

I desperately want to be able to use what I know. I think most people do. I have found that understanding culture and the way it operates is the first step in that process.

Chapter 1

The Root of Culture Wars

There is a way that seems right to a man, but in the end it leads to death.
Proverbs 14:12

Pretend, for a moment, that you are a fish and live in a big lake. As a free swimming, independent resident of the lake, it would be possible for you to swim around and extensively explore every nook and cranny of your underwater environment. Now, that might be a magnificent and worthy project to undertake. In fact, you may become the greatest explorer fish that ever lived in that lake.

In spite of your great exploratory skills, however, there would still be a tremendous amount of the world you could not investigate. Living in a contained body of water, you would be completely cut off from even knowing what existed in the part of the world outside of the area of your lake. For instance, you couldn't go to other, disconnected bodies of water. In fact, you wouldn't even have a way of knowing that they even existed. And, of course, you would have no way of knowing anything about the land areas either.

But say that one day, in the midst of your exploring, you had a great discovery. On that day, as you swam up to the edge of your lake and looked through the surface of the water, you noticed that the land from the lake bottom continued up and out of the lake. There was actually a place which was not underwater.

As you looked through the surface of the water, you could see tall objects that had green tops, and occasionally you even saw various other strange living creatures move in front of you. Since your eyes were designed to be effective underwater, it all seemed rather blurry and distorted, but you could tell something was there.

At that point you would obviously conclude that there is a part of reality which exists beyond your boundaries. But even though you could see it, that nonwatery part of the planet would be an area completely beyond your ability to explore and understand. You have a way to perceive its existence, but there would be a very limited amount of information you could learn about it. Nevertheless, even though your ability to directly explore that area is limited, you are still able to observe around the edges of the lake and make new observations and deductions.

Then, one day, another significant event happened. As you were swimming around, you met a type of fish that you had never seen before. As you went up and talked to him, you found that he had somehow been transported from another lake to yours. Until that point, you had no idea that his species of fish existed, or even that other lakes existed. As he shared with you about his former habitat, you came to realize that there were even different kinds of plant and animal life that didn't exist in your lake. Because of his explanations you could understand much more about the world and about other life forms. Based on that new input, you were able to come up with even more ideas and theories about the nature of the world.

But even taking into account the things you were able to see for yourself through the surface of the water, and the knowledge you gained from that alien fish, your overall understanding about the entirety of the world would still be minuscule. You still wouldn't know anything specific about other bodies of water. You wouldn't know how many other fresh water lakes, rivers, streams and springs existed on the planet or where they were. And you certainly wouldn't have any idea about the large salt water oceans and lakes, which have entirely different properties than your lake—not to mention different life forms. In fact, in your isolated situation, it would be very difficult for you to even conceive of the other places.

The Totality of Reality

This is, basically, the same challenge we face as we live in our material universe. The totality of reality is so much larger than what we can see and explain from our vantage point. There are parts of our universe that we know exist because we can see them with our eyes or at least detect them with our scientific instruments. But much of it we can only observe indirectly or from a distance. There is even more that we simply have to theorize about. In fact, there are probably places that exist which are beyond our ability to detect in any way. Perhaps some of those places have entirely different properties than what we know.

Understanding the material universe, which we can detect and measure, is hard enough, but what about the portion of existence that is outside of the material part? That can only be known if someone from the other part is willing and able to step into our domain and share it with us.

And, in fact, that is exactly what has happened. God has done that as he spoke to prophets, as he came to earth in the form of the man Jesus Christ, and as he spiritually connects with those who choose to enter a relationship with Him. The Bible is the fruit of that revealed truth, but even with that revelation there is still a lot we do not know.

Enough has been revealed to give us a measure of understanding about the totality of existence. This is important because it is only as we understand that unseen part—the spiritual part—that we are able to explore the truth about the life issues in the material world that people have disputes about.

Figuring this out is quite a challenge, but it is possible to make significant progress toward our goal of understanding. To get at it we have to start with what we do know (what we can observe), then move on to try and understand the unseen part (that which has been revealed).

At this point it would be possible for us to talk about the things we have observed through scientific study. We certainly have learned a lot about the internal workings of plant and animal life on the planet. We have been able to explore hidden places on land and in the seas. Our instruments have become so sophisticated that we can even explore microscopic particles. And with telescopes, space ships, and various other instruments, we have even been able to explore some of the far reaches of our universe.

Although this information is valuable, it takes us in a direction that doesn't really help us understand the issues that create culture wars. What we need to explore in order to get at culture issues are human beliefs and the foundations of those beliefs. These areas do, of course, have a physical dimension, so we can't simply ignore the physical element. But a pure scientific evaluation will never give us complete answers to the questions we ask.

We can do some observation and analysis using scientific methods and principles since the outward expressions of beliefs and values are shared in the physical world. But the basis of beliefs and values is spiritual, not physical. As a result we have to quickly move to the disciplines that delve into that area—disciplines such as philosophy and theology.

As we attempt to understand the important issues of the culture war, we will quickly get to the spiritual side of things. But we need to start on the physical level—the tangible things that form the basis for differing cultural expressions. So, what can we observe on a surface level?

Different Strokes for Different Folks

One of the first things we notice about human existence is that there are many different groups of people throughout the world, and each one has its own way of self-expression. Most of the expressions are neither good nor bad in themselves. They are simply *different* ways of doing things. For instance, most Westerners eat noodles with forks while many Easterners use chopsticks. Americans shake hands when they greet each other and Japanese bow. Italians speak Italian, and Germans speak German. Mexicans drive on the right-hand side of the road, and the British drive on the left. You get the idea.

But ethnicity and nationality are not the only kinds of groupings that exist. Most people, in all parts of the world, consider it wrong to go around in public with no clothes on. But nudists have a different set of values which allow for it. They can't express that value among the general population, but in their own nudist colonies they can and do. Homosexuals contend that having a same-sex partner is okay, but most religious faiths consider that to be bad. Most radical feminists consider the choice to have an abortion to be the individual right of a woman, while those who understand life to begin at conception view it as murder.

As can be readily seen, there are a lot of different kinds of groups where a whole variety of different beliefs are expressed. There are nationality groups, age groups, issue groups, social groups, interest groups, ethnic groups, religious groups, political groups, sports groups, professional groups, racial groups, regional groups and on and on. Each of these have beliefs that they follow and particular ways of living out those beliefs in daily life—their own cultures. While there are not huge essential differences between various groups of humans, there are some. These different understandings generate various outward expressions in life.

Some of these expressions reflect differing physical circumstances, such as the language that is spoken or the local climate. But other expressions relate to beliefs and values. And it is these "spiritual" elements, not the physical ones, that cause us to interpret the various parts of our existence as truth or not truth.

We will get deeper into the expressions of beliefs and values in a little bit, but we need to start our journey at the most basic level—the physical expressions of our life situations. By examining the things that we can physically experience, it will be easier for us, then, to move forward and grasp the more abstract issues related to truth.

Digging Deeper

1. What do you believe about the nature of the universe and how does that affect the way you approach living your life?

2. What parts of your culture do you see as good and what parts do you think are bad?

3. What specifically can you do to make a positive influence on the bad parts?

I first got interested in understanding culture when I was thrown into a situation where I actually lived in a culture that was different from my own. That was not, though, my first introduction to the topic. I had studied anthropology, sociology and humanities in college. All of these subjects had given me some background knowledge about the topic. But at that time it all seemed rather esoteric and abstract.

When I actually lived in another culture, though, I experienced firsthand the issues that, before, I had only studied. I actually felt the frustration of not being able to communicate well. I struggled with trying to understand why the people I lived around acted and thought differently than I did.

Cultural differences are not just interesting pieces of information, they are experiential facts of life. The reason this is so important is that our relationships with other people depend on our ability to understand and communicate with them.

I don't know about you, but I want to have relationships with other people. And not just people in my own culture. People in very different cultures have unique things to contribute to my life, as well. And whether the cultures are close or far apart, it is worth it to bridge the gaps for the sake of an expanding web of relationships.

Chapter 2

Culture—The Way People Live

What is man that you are mindful of him, the son of man that you care for him? You made him a little lower than the heavenly beings and crowned him with glory and honor. Psalms 8:4-5

When we first moved to Latvia, I had the opportunity to meet a lot of new people. The folks we got to know were some of the nicest people, and we had a great time making friends. One of the things we enjoyed the most was to entertain people in our home. We often had parties or even just had friends or neighbors over for a meal.

Of course, when people came over, I would greet them at the front door and invite them in. When I first opened the door I would say hello and reach out to shake hands. Shaking hands was a common practice in Latvia so this was not an unusual thing to do, but there was one little quirk. Before they would reach their hand out, they would always jump over the threshold of the door into the house.

At first this really caught me by surprise. I didn't know why they so quickly hopped toward me like that. But I soon found out that they believed it was bad luck to shake hands across the threshold of a door. So, they got on the same side as I was before they shook hands.

Now this little custom was harmless and most people didn't really believe that shaking hands that way would cause bad luck. It was such a pervasive part of the culture, however, that people automatically did it whether they believed in the superstition or not. When I recognized their custom and adapted myself to it, I was able to connect with them at a level that went beyond the mere speaking of words.

As we look at human societies around the world, we see a lot of differences based on gender, skin pigmentation, language, economics and a whole host of other things. People live in many different ways and by all kinds of different standards. But in the midst of all the diversity, we also see many common living patterns. These common group characteristics are referred to as culture.

It is important to understand these different elements because they represent the ways people express themselves. The different expressions embody the matters that are important to various peoples and are the things that we need to be mindful of in order to relate to them personally.

This leads us to the real reason why an understanding of culture is important. *It is the key to relationships.* People identify with those who are like themselves. If we want to relate to people who are different from ourselves, we have to come to some understanding of their culture.

When I lived and worked as a missionary in Japan, it would have been silly for me to expect the Japanese people to adapt to my American ways. Certainly they were curious and liked to ask questions about us, but they were not going to change their way of viewing the world to accommodate me. After all, they were not the ones who felt a calling to get into my life in order to share important beliefs and values. It was the other way around. I was the one who wanted to get into their lives in order to share with them. To do that I had to learn as much as I could about them and their ways of thinking and living. It was necessary for me to identify and learn various aspects of their culture so I could form relationships with them.

Culture can be divided into two basic parts (nonmaterial and material), with each part having multiple elements. Let's begin with a brief definition of these elements.

Non-material Elements of Culture

The nonmaterial elements of culture are those characteristics which define a group of people but which are not physical objects or technological processes. They are things which express the uniqueness and cohesiveness of a particular group. All groups have these elements, but the unique combination is the expression of that group's culture. These elements include the following:

Symbols – Symbols are objects which do not necessarily have significance in and of themselves but have been assigned meaning by the group. They represent ideas or events that are considered important and which help them to establish and maintain their identity as a group. This could include such things as a gesture, a flag or even a statue.

Language – Language is a system of sounds, written symbols and/or gestures that a group of people use to communicate their thoughts and feelings. There are many different spoken and written languages in the world, as well as sign languages.

Values – Values are the standards or judgments that a culture uses to indicate what is good, right or desirable. These standards help to organize the life of the group and are considered inherently worthwhile or desirable. Values might include such concepts as truthfulness, freedom and happiness.

Norms – Norms are the cultural rules which let individuals know how they should behave within the context of their culture. They are the expressions of life that a group considers normal. There are four basic types of norms: folkways, mores, laws and taboos.

> **Folkways** are the weakest level of norms. A culture may consider violation of these to be bad taste or even downright wrong. But they are not seen to be so bad that a harsh penalty would be necessary. For most Americans, such things as having strong body odor or picking your nose in public might be violations of the culture's folkways.

> **Mores** are norms that have a strong meaning. They are the moral beliefs of the group. These rules are considered essential, and society will somehow punish a person who violates them. In American culture, this might include such things as telling the truth or keeping promises.

Laws are a third type of norm. These are things that a culture has decided to officially regulate, and which involve some kind of official sanction if they are violated. There are various levels of laws. The violations of some laws will have harsh consequences while others are quite minor. Driving over the speed limit or engaging in prostitution are examples of actions which have come to be governed by laws in our country.

Taboos are the final category of norms. These are cultural standards which are so strong that to violate them would be considered virtually inconceivable. There may or may not be an official sanction for violating a taboo, but there would certainly be social price to pay. In America, taboos might include such things as cannibalism or public nudity.

Material Elements of Culture

Material elements of culture are physical objects and technological processes which characterize the daily life of a group of people. These are elements which can be seen and manipulated. Many of the material elements of any given culture will be common to numerous other cultures, but most groups will have some physical components which are unique to them.

Technology – Technology is the body of knowledge that members of a group apply to their physical environment in order to meet their comfort and survival needs. Certain needs arise and people develop ways to meet the needs. These processes can include such things as the use of utensils to eat with, like a fork or chopsticks, or the use of a computer to write a letter.

Artifacts – Artifacts are the physical objects that a society makes in order to apply their technology. Using the examples above concerning utensils, every society needs to eat so they have developed technologies for eating. The actual objects that are used for eating are the artifacts. The unique cultural expression comes about as you look at the particular shape, material or design properties of the artifacts.

Keeping Culture in Perspective

Many people view their own culture as the standard by which every other person or group should be judged. It is the way they were raised and is, of course, "the right way" to view and live life.

Within any single culture, there are certainly things that are right and which people in every other culture should be willing to imitate. But the "right" things exist, not because they are elements of any particular culture, but because they are consistent with a greater truth that exists beyond physical culture. There are also things within any given culture which are bad because they are inconsistent with truth.

It is good for us to analyze and understand our own culture and the cultures of others. It is good because it gives us a better perspective on life. *But the main reason it is important is that it gives us connecting points by which we are able to make relationships with other people.* Relationship requires that there be something in common.

When we go beyond simply connecting with others and begin to make evaluations about individuals or groups based strictly on our own culture, we are setting ourselves up for a life that is narrowminded and that shuts out the possibility for us to grasp the greater truth. *That greater truth is that there are objective principles which exist beyond all cultural expressions.*

As we consider the culture war that is being fought in the world today, what we are really seeing is the clash that arises out of the conflicting beliefs of various groups. One group thinks that displaying the Ten Commandments in public buildings is promoting religion, while another group believes that it is simply a recognition of the historical fact that the American system of laws was based on the Decalogue. One group believes that profanity on TV is perfectly okay, while another group believes that it is offensive.

When opposing groups try to promote their own agendas, what we usually see is a fierce battle over the cultural objects themselves. One group is trying to put the Ten Commandments on the wall, and the other one trying to take them down. One group is going to court to argue that profanity on TV is a First Amendment right and the other is arguing for stiff fines against a moral offender. These clashes in the public arena are inevitable. You can't get around them because the two different points of view can't exist side by side. Either the commandments are there or they are not. Either profanity is used or it is not.

But the real war is not the culture war. These outward expressions are indications of something else. They are expressions of beliefs and values that are the foundation of the outward expressions. To effectively deal with the outward expressions, we have to understand the underlying beliefs. Let's move on, now, and take the next step as we try to understand what the possible belief systems are and where they come from.

Digging Deeper

1.   What parts of your culture make it easy for you to make relationships with others who are of your same culture?

2.   What parts of your culture make it difficult for you to make relationships with others who are of a different culture?

3.   What are some of the big issues that are creating tension within your culture today?

I first entered into a personal relationship with God through faith in Jesus Christ when I was sixteen years old, although I had been going to church much longer than that. My parents were church-going people, and we had been active as far back as I can remember.

But everything changed when I personally met God. What had previously been merely a weekly activity suddenly became a very personal and deeply spiritual journey.

I also remember a period of time, two or three years after that, while I was in college. I was in an anthropology class taught by a teacher who did not believe in God. This person explained all of life, and cultural development, in terms of evolutionary processes—all without a need for God.

I didn't realize, at the time, what was happening. All I knew was that what I was being taught was radically different than what I had experienced at age sixteen. This conflict of ideas created a great deal of inner turmoil for me and made me even question whether or not there really was a God.

What I know now is that the struggle I was dealing with was the clash of two worldviews within my mind. That began my journey to discover the truth about worldview—a journey that has profoundly strengthened my faith.

Chapter 3

Worldview—The Way People Think

Now to him who is able to establish you by my gospel and the proclamation of Jesus Christ, according to the revelation of the mystery hidden for long ages past, but now revealed and made known through the prophetic writings by the command of the eternal God, so that all nations might believe and obey him. Romans 16:25-26

I remember when I was a kid and used to play golf out in my yard. I don't know what attracted me to it. When I got a little older and tried to really learn how to play I was horrible—so bad, in fact, that I finally came to the conclusion that I would be better served putting my energies into a different sport. But when I was a kid, I really did have a good time with it. I would get my dad's golf clubs out, make some holes in various spots around the yard and play.

In his bag he always kept some golf balls that were pretty ragged. In fact, with the covers split open and the insides exposed, those balls were almost unusable. One day my curiosity got the best of me, and I took out one of those torn-up balls and ripped the cover off. The core was very hard and wrapped with what looked like rubber bands. It was designed to have properties that would make it go a long way when it was hit with a golf club.

I have seen the insides of other kinds of balls, too. The insides of a football and basketball are empty; they are just rubber bladders that hold air. The insides of some softballs are made with a cork material. The various balls used in different sports are designed with particular properties that allow people to play the games. Can you imagine a football with the insides of a golf ball? Somebody would get killed! Can you imagine a golf ball that had the insides of a basketball? I don't know what it would play like, but the game of golf would become something entirely different than it is now. *The inside makes all the difference.*

15

Culture Is Simply What
We See on the Outside

The reason we took the time in the previous chapter to define the various elements of culture, was because when we look at what is going on in the world, culture is what we see. It is the outward, tangible expression of human activity.

From here we could start digging into the different aspects of culture and analyze them to death, but that is not the intention of this book. That would be like doing a detailed examination of the covers of the different balls. You could find out a lot about certain aspects of the balls, but you would never understand why they act the way they do. Just like with the balls, it is the inside properties of societies that determine how the game of life is able to be played. *We have to strip the cultural expressions off to get at the underlying issues.*

It has already been noted that there are many aspects of every culture that have nothing to do with what is right and wrong, real and unreal. We will leave the exploration of those material expressions of culture to the anthropologists. What we are interested in are the expressions of culture which are related to values and norms—the things which define what is right and what is wrong, real and unreal.

It is obvious that not every way of looking at life can be right. We have already mentioned some beliefs held by various groups which totally contradict one another. To move toward our goal of understanding the culture war we are fighting, we have to head in a different direction.

Belief Systems

There is actually something that exists which underlies cultures. These underlying foundations are the belief systems from which cultures emerge. It seems that whatever someone believes is somehow expressed outwardly in culture. You do what you believe, and you don't do what you don't believe. For instance a person is not born with a gene that forces them have to have sexual relations outside of marriage. Yet there are some groups who believe this to be okay, and they approve of it for members of their culture.

This belief about sexuality is not a necessary part of any culture. In fact, there will be individuals, even within a culture, that accept sexual relations outside of marriage and do not follow the prevailing cultural trends. And if we step back even further and look at a broader spectrum of cultural groups, we will find entire cultures which believe just the opposite. The actions are not the beliefs—they are only the tangible expressions of the beliefs. To learn the real beliefs of an individual, we have to work backwards from the actions. Your belief system defines your life purpose, and you take action to fulfill that purpose.

So where do these beliefs come from? For most people they are not carefully thought out ideas—they just exist. They come from a set of assumptions about the nature of reality that we pick up from the environment we were raised in. From this way of thinking emerge the actions that we take.

What Is a Worldview?

There are some very powerful life mechanisms that emerge out of culture. But the cultural properties, themselves, are only outward expressions of an underlying set of beliefs we call worldview.

A worldview is a set of assumptions about the way reality is structured. Notice the word assumption. For most people, these assumptions are never analyzed and are often not even consciously known. They are like a filter through which we view the world. It is possible to analyze the filter, but most people are so focused on the world they are seeing through it that the filter itself is not even considered. But different filters cause things to appear differently, so it is essential to know which one is being used in order to understand how our view of life is being affected.

Consider, for a moment, the different kinds of lens filters that can be used on a camera. If you put on a filter that is blue, for instance, all of the color blue is filtered out. As you look through the lens, your perception of colors will be skewed. Now, if you had lived your whole life looking through a lens with a blue filter and had never seen the world without it, you might think that the coloring you were looking at was normal. But in actual fact that would not be true.

17

How about another filter—a fisheye lens. This very wide angle lens allows you to view much more of a scene than you would be able to see with the naked eye. The only problem is, with a fisheye lens, proportion is grossly distorted. But what if that were all you had ever known? You could think even something that far off was normal.

Our worldview works like that as it relates to our beliefs and our understanding about the way life is organized. If you were taught all your life that one particular way of believing, or of analyzing the world, was the correct way, you would believe it even if it wasn't true. You might not even realize that there were other possibilities. There is something (some perspective) that is true. But if we were not brought up to believe that way, our understanding of the nature of our existence would be different regardless of the real truth.

For instance, I have had people express to me very strong opinions about which version of the Bible is the best one. As I listened to their arguments, it became clear that their reasoning had nothing to do with a deliberate analysis of the subject. It is just that they had grown up all their lives hearing that one particular version was good and, for various reasons, others were bad. No matter how well reasoned a counter argument was constructed, these people refused to consider another possibility. They are married to their assumptions. It is not because they have thought it out or studied it. Rather, it is because those assumptions have become a part of their worldview and cannot be questioned.

We can still live with a false worldview, but there are certainly going to be things that we miss out on. The most important issues we must deal with in life do not pertain to how we relate to the physical world; they relate to spiritual/eternal issues. Misunderstandings of physical reality impact our physical lives. But a misunderstanding of the nature of the spiritual world affects our physical lives here and now, as well as our interaction with eternity. It is at this point that analyzing our assumptions and getting our worldview right becomes critical.

So, just what are the issues that relate to worldview? There are several ways to get at this, but Dr. James Sire, in his book, *The Universe Next Door*, spells it out in a way that, to me, is the easiest to understand. He does this by asking seven basic questions that elicit the beliefs of the various worldviews.

1. What is the most fundamental reality? (Ultimate reality)
2. What is the nature of our material reality? (Material reality)
3. What is a human being? (Humanity)
4. What happens to a person at death? (Death)
5. Why is it possible to know anything at all? (Knowledge)
6. How do we know what is right and wrong? (Morality)
7. What is the meaning of human history? (History)

To put this into perspective, every worldview is going to have its own way of answering these questions. A New-Ager will answer them differently than a Christian, who will answer them differently than a Hindu, who will answer them differently than an atheist, and so on.

Just by looking at the questions it becomes obvious that there are a huge number of possible ways to answer the questions, and people actually do answer them in different ways. Some of those ways are even quite contradictory. Those different answers generate different ways of constructing culture.

Since these questions form the very essence of a person's understanding of how life is organized, they are very strongly held. Is it any wonder that the cultural expressions which emerge out of them are also strongly held and that clashes of cultures occur?

It is one thing to understand the principle of how this works, but we need to go a step further to get at the specifics. Let's take a look at the basic worldview categories and begin to fill in the blanks as to why culture conflicts exist.

Digging Deeper

1. Take a few moments to answer the seven worldview questions for yourself.
2. How do your answers to these questions affect the way you live your life?

All of the major worldviews can be found, to some extent, in America, today. But there are two that highly influence the vast majority of the population and are the root of the culture wars we see going on in this country. Perhaps the most graphic evidence of the conflict is seen as we look at the political map and observe the "red state - blue state" divide. Not that the culture war itself is political, but the political divide is one dramatic expression of it.

I remember learning the theory of evolution in high school biology. These days there is a huge debate going on about how to teach it. Should the arguments *against* evolution be taught alongside the arguments for it? It is a theory, after all.

But back in my day, this discussion was not prominent. Evolution was called a theory, but was taught as if it were fact. I remember questioning my biology teacher, but I was at a huge disadvantage. After all I was just a sophomore in high school, and the teacher had her masters degree in biological sciences from college.

I had to do a lot of independent study to get my deeper questions answered about evolution. In the meantime, it created a great deal of mental anguish for me. I know that this particular struggle has been a common one for several generations.

Chapter 4

What Are the Basic Worldviews?

Trust in the LORD with all your heart and lean not on your own under-standing; in all your ways acknowledge him, and he will make your paths straight. Proverbs 3:5-6

When I was a missionary in Latvia, I developed a website to tell people about my family and my work. On the website I also had a section that shared the basics of my faith. And, of course, I also listed an e-mail address so that people who wanted to contact me could do so.

You never know who will look at a website and make contact. One day I got an e-mail from a guy in New York who saw the website and decided to write. The reason he wrote was because he read the section about my faith and wanted to let me know that I was stupid to believe that Jesus Christ was God in the flesh.

Well, I decided to engage him (nicely, of course) and wrote him a return e-mail. I addressed the points he made and asked him how he knew his point of view was right. His reply was, "That is what my professors in college taught me, and they should know."

I replied again that I disagreed with him and asked him how he knew his professors were right. After all, there are many people, even other professors, who take a different point of view.

He never could get past that point. He didn't have an answer for me, but wasn't willing to concede that there was any way his teachers could be wrong. He was stuck and, after a final, nasty e-mail, simply quit corresponding.

Why did he contact me in the first place, then end it the way he did? The reason was that what he read on my website contradicted his religion. Now in this man's case, religion did not include God, al-though it was his religion just the same. He had a set of faith assump-

21

tions about the way reality is organized and could not stand to see another faith put into the public square. Then, when he couldn't answer questions posed by the other faith, he ran away from it.

In a very real sense, our worldview is our religion. It is the underlying set of beliefs upon which we build our entire understanding of life.

In one sense it could be argued that there are billions of worldviews. In fact, each individual has a distinct perspective on life and sees things in a slightly different way than every other person on the planet. But that is way too diverse an approach to come to any kind of understanding. We need some way to group similar points of view.

As we look a little more closely, we can see that, in spite of the great diversity, there are some common groupings that do exist. In fact, there are a relatively limited number of fundamental worldview categories. This is really where we must start—with the big picture. After that, each category can be broken down into other major or minor sub-categories until we finally get down to individual, personal beliefs.

Different people break these categories down in various ways, but for our purposes we will try to start as broadly as possible. The major categories we will look at are Naturalism, Animism, Far Eastern Thought and Theism. After we look at their basic underlying belief structures, we can begin to understand the many ways these are expressed outwardly in culture. To get a good overview of the different worldviews, we will give a short background explanation of each one followed by an account of how they answer the seven worldview questions.

Naturalism

Some people might look at the word "naturalism" and think it has something to do with nature religions. It is actually quite different than that. The ideas behind naturalism date back to ancient times but began to emerge as a widely accepted way to understand life in the 17th and 18th centuries. It made its big splash on the philosophical stage when Darwin connected this philosophy with physical science. Once that link was made, other thinkers began to apply the worldview concepts to additional areas such as law, psychology, sociology, anthropology, religion and so on.

A number of different ideologies have spun off from naturalism—beliefs such as nihilism, existentialism, new age (to a degree), secular humanism, positivism, atheism, and many expressions of postmodernism. Each of these ideologies takes off in different directions and comes to different conclusions about the way the universe operates, but naturalism is their basic starting point.

Basic Worldview Beliefs of Naturalism

Ultimate reality: The basic premise of naturalism is that the only thing which exists is matter. There is no God and there is nothing outside of the material universe.

Material reality: Matter itself is considered to be eternal and, through the eternal operation of natural laws by evolutionary processes, it has formed itself into the universe we know today.

Humanity: Human beings are simply complex biological machines. Human personality is real enough but is not a special creation, so there is no particular meaning associated with it. It is simply what happens when a brain develops to the level of complexity that the human brain has attained.

Death: When death occurs, the individual life form simply ceases to exist. There is no spiritual dimension and no afterlife.

Knowledge: The ability of human beings to reason and gain intellectual insight was just a chance happening through natural evolutionary processes.

Morality: Since humans did evolve with the ability to reason and to be self-aware, ethics and morality emerged as issues to be dealt with. To the naturalist, however, the ethical systems of humans have no basis in ultimate reality and there is no foundation for an ethical code based outside of the material world. Humanity decides for itself what is right or wrong based on what the individual or a particular group feels is best for them.

History: Since naturalists don't acknowledge any existence outside of material reality, history becomes nothing more than a stream of events moving in a straight line from the past to the future. Since man has the ability to reason and to be self-aware, he can recognize patterns in this historical stream, but they are nothing more than a series of cosmic accidents.

Animism

The primary belief of animism is that there are many spirit beings who exist in the universe. Some are seen to inhabit material objects (like trees and rocks), some are heavenly objects (sky, sun, moon, stars), some are animals, and others are the spirits of people who have died. Animism tends to be centered more in primitive societies and pagan religions.

For the animist, interaction with various spiritual beings is vital, and prayers and offerings are given to win their good will. These spiritual beings have various dispositions—some are looking out for the interests of humanity while others are malicious. It is up to living humans to perform rituals and give offerings in order to manipulate and placate these gods for their own purposes.

Basic Worldview Beliefs of Animism

Ultimate Reality & Material Reality: Animists see the universe as containing both material and immaterial elements. Spirit beings are considered to exist in a separate dimension but also operate in, and have influence over, the material universe. Their activities affect the lives of humans—for good or evil. The spirit beings (or gods) have limited power and work with material that already exists.

Humanity: To animists, humans are simply material creatures who inhabit this world. They also have the ability to interact with spirit beings.

Death: Upon physical death each person will become a spirit being and live in the realm of the spirits.

Knowledge: Knowledge is just assumed to exist. Humans live in the world, observe its operation and live life based on those observations.

Morality: The concepts of right and wrong are primarily based on experience—both personal and group experience. The underlying idea is to try and avoid things which cause other people, or the gods, to give you problems in life. If bad things begin happening, you can assume that there has been an offense against some god that must be righted. Over time, animist societies have come to a collective understanding of the basic nature of these "rights and wrongs" and of what must be done to correct the wrongs. Usually a priest or shaman is the one who knows how to discern the problems and effectively deal with the gods.

History: History, for the animist, is seen primarily as a linear progression of events but without any underlying meaning. People can learn from it but it does not lead to any particular cosmic conclusion.

Far Eastern Thought

Far Eastern Thought takes the view that reality is a single impersonal "thing," and everything, in every part of existence, is a part of that ultimate reality. This understanding of the nature of existence originated, and is most prominent, in the Far East. The primary belief systems which incorporate these ideas are Hinduism, Buddhism and some elements of the New Age movement. Far Eastern Thought does not distinguish between the secular and the divine—everything is god and god is everything. It also sees all of reality as composed of, and reducible to, a single substance. Everything that exists is simply a different form of the same basic material.

Basic Worldview Beliefs of Far Eastern Thought

Ultimate Reality: This worldview teaches that reality consists of a nonmaterial part and a material part, and both parts emerge out of the same substance. The ultimate goal of every creature in the material

world is to progress through successive lives (by the process of reincarnation) and to ultimately escape the material arena and become totally absorbed into the immaterial cosmos. When this happens a
person ceases to exist as an individual and becomes part of the whole.
Everything that exists is part of a larger whole—an ultimate reality
which is God. This ultimate reality is understood to be infinite and
impersonal.

Material Reality: Far Eastern thought is built on the idea that there is
a single reality which covers both what we are able to experience as
well as that which is beyond our experience. Some things are just
closer to being "at one with the One" (absorbed into the immaterial
cosmos). The things that are closest to the One are unseen reality,
while things further away appear to us as the material world.
Individual creatures pass through a series of lives and are constantly
seeking to cycle to higher and higher levels. The ultimate goal is to
move out of the material part and reach the place where one can be
absorbed fully into the One. Ultimately, all roads lead to the One.

Humanity: Humans may appear to be personal and individual but
that is an illusion. Everything is an expression of the great impersonal
One, and that includes humanity. The human perception that some
things are personal is an illusion.

Death: When death comes, it is the end of an individual living being's
personal existence but not the end of its essential nature. When a
person dies, the life force simply recycles (reincarnates) into another
form on the path to becoming fully a part of the whole.

Knowledge: Knowledge is virtually a meaningless concept. When individuals realize their oneness with the cosmos, they have passed beyond knowledge. In the realm of ultimate reality, what we appear to
know does not really exist as it appears. We cannot know anything for
certain in this existence and, when we understand that we cannot
know anything, we move to the next level of understanding and experience.

Morality: The same principle applies to the concept of morality. The cosmos is seen to be perfect at every moment. When an individual realizes his or her oneness with the cosmos, that individual passes beyond good and evil. What appears to be good and evil in the material world is not the nature of true reality.

History: Time is also an illusion. Everything exists in the state of eternity. Time moves in cycles, not in a linear progression. It moves from one life to the next in the process of advancing toward oneness with the One. When individuals realize their oneness with the One, they pass beyond time.

Theism

Theism teaches that there is an actual, infinite and transcendent God who created the material order. Within the major theme of Theism, there are quite a number of variations, including Christianity, Judaism and Islam. There are also many spin-offs of these major groups such as Jehovah's Witnesses, Mormons and the Moonies, just to name a few. Generally speaking, theistic groups depend on some kind of revelation to support their positions.

Basic Worldview Beliefs of Theism

Ultimate Reality: Theism acknowledges an infinite and transcendent God who is the Creator and Sustainer of the material universe. In its various forms, God may be understood as either personal or impersonal.

Material Reality: God intentionally created the material universe and made it to operate on the basis of cause and effect. The universe is seen to have a definite natural order. Most theistic systems, but not all, believe it is possible for God to intervene and alter the course of events in the physical universe as he sees fit.

Humanity: Human beings are acknowledged to be a special creation of God. They are a special order that is significantly different from other created beings and have both a material part and a spiritual part.

Because of the spiritual part, mankind is able to have some kind of interaction with, and knowledge of, God.

Death: Death is not considered the extinction of life but the transferring of life, in a different form, to an eternal existence outside of material reality—either heaven or hell.

Knowledge: Mankind is able to have knowledge about the world and about eternal reality because God created human beings with that ability. To enhance this natural ability, God also actively communicates with humanity to impart knowledge. This communication comes in the form of various types of revelation.

Morality: Because this revelation from God exists, humans are able to have a strong sense of ethics and morality. God, himself, has revealed what is right and wrong.

History: History is understood to operate in a linear fashion as a meaningful succession of events. It began with a creative act of God and is moving toward the ultimate fulfillment of God's purposes for the world.

Does All of This Really Mean Anything?

There are literally billions of people who adhere to each of the basic worldviews. And, as we look around the world to see the plight of most of these people, it is obvious that a lot of folks are searching for truth and meaning in their lives. As sad as it is, a lot of the expressions of that searching results in hatred, warfare and intolerance based on strongly held beliefs. Unfortunately, that trouble spills over, through various cultural expressions, into the lives of individuals all over the globe.

But that is not all. The places where those expressions bump up against other worldviews also create massive amounts of conflict. For these reasons, an understanding of worldview has great significance, both on an individual level and as human societies interact with each other.

Digging Deeper

1.   Take a moment to read through the various beliefs in each of the worldviews. Which ones in each of the worldviews do you agree or have sympathy with?

2.   Which single worldview most closely aligns with your own beliefs?

3.   How can knowing the basic beliefs of the various worldviews help you in your life?

I suppose at some point in life, every one of us faces a crisis of faith. These crises happen in moments when we face the choice to live life by what we know is right or to compromise our beliefs and go in a different direction. I know I have had times when I struggled with this.

Many times the crisis relates to a moral decision. Will I participate in pre-marital or extra-marital sex? Will I cheat on an exam? Will I shoplift a CD from the store?

Other times the crisis happens when the belief system we grew up believing gets challenged for the first time by another one that also seems to make sense. This often happens in high school or college classes or even by watching certain movies or TV shows.

The solution that I have found to this problem is to have a very clear and conscious understanding of the basics of my own belief system. There is such a thing as absolute truth, and when it is clearly and effectively put up alongside beliefs that are not truth, the contrast becomes obvious. The main problem is, we don't often see it demonstrated that way. In fact, every worldview has a vested interest in maximizing its appearance of truth and minimizing its points of deviation.

I believe that Relational Revelation is the truth. And when it is clearly put side-by-side with other worldviews, it just makes more sense.

Chapter 5

Relational Revelation— A Special Worldview

For God so loved the world that he gave his one and only Son, that whoever believes in him shall not perish but have eternal life. For God did not send his Son into the world to condemn the world, but to save the world through him. 18 Whoever believes in him is not condemned, but whoever does not believe stands condemned already because he has not believed in the name of God's one and only Son. John 3:16-18

Before we move forward to the next step and explore how worldview expresses itself in culture, there is one other worldview category that we need to explore. It is a specialized form of theism which makes a unique contribution to our ability to understand the truth of our existence.

One of the big debates in science and religion has to do with the origin of the universe. These days, the Big Bang theory seems to be all the rage. This is the theory that at some point in history all the material stuff in the entire physical universe existed in a single, very dense ball of matter and energy. Somehow that mass exploded and the material was blown in every direction. It ended up being grouped in bunches that became galaxies, stars, planetary systems, comets and so on.

Naturalists believe that over time, after the bang occurred, natural forces like gravity, nuclear reactions, etc., caused the universe, as we know it, to evolve into what it is today. Their belief is that everything can be explained by natural means. They point to the "big bang" to establish their creation myth.

The big problem that they run into, though, is that they are not able to say where the mass of matter came from to form the big bang. Everyone knows that one of the basic principles of science is that matter cannot emerge out of nothing. It can change forms, but not simply appear out of nothing. But naturalism has to have some explanation for this. So some naturalists say, "We just don't yet know." Others contend that matter itself is eternal.

Now I want to know something. Where does that idea come from that matter could be eternal? It is not a scientific statement! And to top that off, it doesn't line up at all with the underlying assumptions of science. No one can point to any kind of scientific data or research that indicates matter is eternal. Rather, it is a faith assumption. The underlying faith assumption is that all of existence can be explained by natural means. That being the case, a naturalist must assume that there is a mechanical explanation for the existence of all matter. Even with no evidence, that is the only possibility which is considered.

Animists and believers in Far Eastern thought don't really deal so much with the issue of origins. Some of them do have creation stories, but they come across more like fairytale myths than as something that actually happened.

Most theistic belief systems, on the other hand, believe that there is a God who exists outside of the natural universe and who created material reality out of nothing. This means that there is more than one dimension of existence.

So which view matches up most closely with how we perceive reality? In a general sense, Theism provides the best explanation for the way we experience the real world. It allows us to account for the way material reality works based on our scientific understanding, yet also gives us a category to reasonably understand the things that go beyond where science can reach.

But there is still one problem that we must come to grips with. There are quite a number of versions of theism, and each of them have characteristics which contradict all the others. So not only do we need to filter through to find which basic worldview is most viable, we also need to discover which version of the best worldview matches up most closely with our understanding of the way reality operates.

Relational Revelation—A Special Worldview

In order to provide a foundation for understanding this topic, we have had to give some cursory explanations of different worldviews. But we haven't gone into a lot of detail because that is not the purpose of this book. There are others who have written extensively about this subject and you can research that topic more fully with them.

Our purpose, here, is more basic. All we want to do is provide a solid platform for you to stand on so that you will have a means of digging deeper into the subject. Because of that, we will now simply cut to the chase and lay out the specific version of theism that seems to most closely match up with the evidence found throughout the history of mankind, and with the way human beings experience reality. This one also gives the most reasonable explanation (though it is also a faith statement) of how the material universe came into being.

This particular form of theism is special and unique. It is the pattern that is commonly expressed as Evangelical Christianity. But, for this book, I want to give it a different name to distinguish it even further. In fact, I want to coin a new term. I will call this form of theism Relational Revelation. It is relational because it acknowledges the importance of an intimate and personal relationship with God, and because God himself provided the means by which the relationship could happen through the life and work of Jesus Christ. It is revelational because it confesses that the Bible (both Old and New Testaments) was given directly to mankind by God in order to reveal himself, his ways and his desires.

Those who agree with me will find what follows to be somewhat familiar, and perhaps comfortable. But don't think that there is nothing for you to gain if you tend toward a different set of beliefs, or are not sure. Even if you don't think you agree with the views written here, there are several important things you will gain by continuing on.

First, you will come to an understanding that you, too, have worldview assumptions that are based on something. You will be a more grounded person if you ever figure out what that is.

Secondly, there are a lot of people in the world who believe in Relational Revelation. You will become more knowledgeable about

33

the beliefs of a very large group of people if you acquire this understanding.

Thirdly, relationships with people are important for society. You can't relate effectively to people you don't understand. Understanding the underlying beliefs of those whose worldview is Relational Revelation will help you become more effective in every area of life that requires interacting with people.

Finally, even though the beliefs of Relational Revelation are in the forefront, here, you will also gain some understanding of the other belief systems that exist in the world. You interact with people from those systems, as well.

Basic Worldview Beliefs of Relational Revelation

We have already touched on the general underlying beliefs of theism and of this particular branch of it. For the purpose of additional clarity, let's look specifically at how Relational Revelation deals with the worldview questions.

Ultimate Reality: Relational Revelation teaches that God is infinite (meaning that he is self-existent, self-conscious, reflective and self-determinate), personal (he interacts with humanity on a personal level), transcendent (beyond our ability to fully know him), omniscient (all knowing), sovereign (in complete control), good (expressed as holy— absolutely no wrong or evil in him), righteous (must judge all evil) and love (he especially formulated a way for flawed humanity to personally interact with himself).

Material Reality: God created the universe out of nothing as an open system (a system where it is possible for the material and spiritual to interact), and he does insert himself into the affairs of the world in ways that go beyond the physical laws of nature when it suits his purpose. The universe has a definite order but it is not completely preprogramed. It is possible for decisions made by God and man to alter the course of events within the boundaries of God's overall plan.

Humanity: Human beings are understood to be creatures created in the image of God and thus we possess the qualities that God possesses—qualities such as personality, self-transcendence, intelligence, morality, creativity and the ability to communicate. As a result, God is not like man. Rather, man is like God (only not having these characteristics to the degree that God has them).

Death: Death is not seen as extinction, but as the transporting of life to an eternal existence outside of material reality in either heaven or hell.

Knowledge: Humanity is able to have knowledge about the world because God has built into each person the ability to learn and to know. In addition to the knowledge we are able to gain by living and interacting in the material world, we are also able to know some things about God because he is personal and is actively engaged in communicating with humanity to impart this knowledge. These communications take the form of various types of revelation.

Morality: Knowledge of right and wrong is also a part of the revelation from God. The Revelation teaches that God created the world to operate under a fixed set of laws—both physical and moral. A sense of moral understanding is also an inherent part of our being that we often identify as conscience. A decision to disregard physical law brings obvious consequences. But God's moral law is an objective reality, as well, and those choosing not to live according to it will suffer separation from him.

History: Finally, history is seen as a meaningful sequence of events that began with a creative act of God. In the course of history, God has interjected himself in ways that allow mankind to know him in a personal relationship. This is particularly evident in the birth, life, death and resurrection of Jesus Christ. History is moving toward an ultimate fulfillment of God's purposes for humanity. At some point the material portion of reality will cease to exist as it is now known and be transformed into a "new earth" that ultimately fulfills God's purpose for the creation.

Our Interest

The reason we need to be interested in culture and worldview is because each worldview and each expression of culture has a starting place which leads to a particular conclusion. Most lead to conclusions that will ultimately take a culture to destruction—either by causing it to spiral down a path which leads to anarchy (as seen by anarchistic demonstrators at many events involving world leaders) or by creating a rigid society where freedom of choice and action are eliminated (as evidenced by nearly every Communist or Fascist government that has ever existed).

We, indeed, have an interest in finding the right worldview expression and in living it out radically in an earthly culture. But we also have to go about it the right way. People will not change the way they live without a compelling inner reason to do so. We can easily identify what we consider evil parts of every cultural group on earth and attack those elements. But our personal beliefs are not going to be convincing to those who believe that the things we call evil are actually good. And when we start promoting the Christian worldview, they will not stand idly by and watch us eliminate things they like or want. And even if we were able to eliminate certain "bad" behaviors, they would reemerge as other people appear who still believe in those behaviors. All you have to do is to look back at the Prohibition episode to see that this is true.

The only way lasting change is going to happen is as individuals have an inner change—a change of worldview. They have to come to a new understanding of the best way to live life.

It is possible to give a reasoned argument for any and every worldview—and there are scores of books that have been written to do just that (I hope you will take the time to study the resources listed in the appendix of this book and begin that personal investigation for yourself). But our purpose, here, is a bit more basic. It is to help us develop a solid understanding of the true nature of our existence and to use that knowledge to propel our lives, and our culture, forward.

There is a way that reality objectively exists. I believe we can actually get a handle on it, but only if we look at life through a worldview lens that lets us see it. When we get to the point where we analyze the bottom line, there is only one worldview that allows us to understand reality as it actually is—Relational Revelation. It leads us to understand that the ultimate expression of culture is the culture of the Kingdom of God. This culture, though, is not a material culture—it is spiritual. It does, however, play out in material life. Kingdom culture produces a particular way of doing relationships, morality, lifestyle and attitude which forms an outward cultural expression. This expression is able to operate within the bounds of all earthly cultures. It is the way God intends for mankind to live life.

In the process of understanding the various worldviews, it is important to have a sense of the basic underlying beliefs of each one. We have taken the time to do that. Now, we need to do one more thing. We need to have just a little more understanding of how each worldview actually plays out in life as it is lived day by day.

Digging Deeper

1.   Look at the way that Relational Revelation answers each of the seven worldview questions. What do you agree with and what do you disagree with? To the best of your ability, explain why you agree or disagree.

2.   If you completely followed through by living life based on Relational Revelation, what would be different about the way you live daily life?

3.   What problem(s) do you have with the beliefs of Relational Revelation and what would be required to solve those problems?

I believe that just about everyone wants to have their own way. As I think about my family, I see this played out virtually every day. Sometimes I have to work really hard to get to the TV set and start watching my show before my wife or son comes in. Whoever gets there first, and establishes control of the remote, determines what program will be on the tube.

Actually, we have all gotten pretty good at figuring out what shows we want to watch, so we don't often have any serious conflicts. But once in a while there are two shows on at the same time that different people want to watch, and we argue about who will have priority.

It is impossible, with the technology in our house, to have both shows going at the same time, so somebody wins and somebody loses. Since two people can't get what they want simultaneously, a choice is made and a specific outcome plays itself out in life.

Worldview is like that. We all have a worldview that we live by. The one each of us has chosen excludes every other one. If we change our worldview, we take on a new one and the old one is gone. Our new choice is played out in life by the way we live.

Chapter 6

How the Basic Worldviews Are Played Out in Culture

Do not be deceived: God cannot be mocked. A man reaps what he sows. The one who sows to please his sinful nature, from that nature will reap destruction; the one who sows to please the Spirit, from the Spirit will reap eternal life. Galatians 6:7-8

I was listening to talk radio recently and the discussion had to do with the legitimacy of the war in Iraq. Since this was a conservative talk show, obviously the view of the host was that the war was just and that the objective of the war was to create a solid base of democracy in the Middle East that would influence the rest of the region.

Often the hosts of those kinds of shows like to have callers of a "liberal" persuasion since it creates controversy and keeps the listeners more engaged. This was one of those times when a liberal caller phoned in and started talking about how the war was unjust and that it wasn't accomplishing anything but getting our soldiers killed.

The call actually went on for about five minutes with the caller and the host going back and forth stating their positions. In this particular instance, both people kept making the same points over and over again. I don't believe either one of them ever got the point of the other. Certainly neither one convinced the other. As I listened, it sometimes seemed that they were not even talking about the same subject. The dialogue went something like this.

Caller: This war is totally unjustified and is not accomplishing anything but getting our boys killed.
Host: What do you mean unjustified? Don't you realize that after 9/11 we had to go after these guys?

Caller: The Iraqis don't even want us over there. The U.S. isn't accomplishing anything.
Host: We are rooting out the people who want to kill Americans and
setting up a stable government that will fight against terrorism.
Caller: Trying to set up a democracy goes against their whole history.
That is not what they want.
Host: When elections are held and a new government is formed, it
will put great pressure on the other Middle Eastern governments who
have been helping terrorists.

And the call kept going on just like that. Both of their underlying
notions were so far away from the other that it was like they were not
even talking to each other.

That is what happens when worldviews collide. Everyone lives
their lives based on how they answer the worldview questions. When
two people who answer them differently try to interact with each
other regarding issues that grow out of worldview, it is almost as if they
were talking different languages.

All we have done so far is to spell out the fact that several major
belief systems express themselves tangibly in the world—the various
expressions of culture. We have also established that there are underlying sets of assumptions behind every culture that are called worldviews. Now let's take a moment to look a little more closely at the
various worldviews to see what kinds of cultural expressions logically
emerge from each one, and why they do, or do not, match up with the
way we humans experience life.

As we look at the following explanations, it must be remembered
that we are only talking broad categories, here—more or less the
"pure" belief set. These broad categories are "types" which have many,
many variations. Within each worldview category are huge variations
even to the point where conflicting, and even contradictory, beliefs
exist within a single worldview. There are people who believe in God
but are also committed naturalists. There are people who identify
themselves as Christians but believe in reincarnation. There are naturalists who believe in God, and so on. The following explanations are
simply designed to give us a sense of where the basic worldviews lead.

Naturalism

In Naturalism there is no such thing as an objective right and wrong, good and evil. When a culture goes about creating its various values and norms, they are strictly functional elements. When a group forms, and as it evolves, an overall consensus develops as to the kinds of values and behaviors that will be useful for the survival of the group. If the conditions or situations change, there is no compelling reason why the cultural elements can't also be changed. Morality is simply what the group wants it to be or what it finds useful for its survival.

The use of technology and artifacts are also impacted. There is nothing innately good or bad, right or wrong about the use of any process or object, except as the culture defines it. When any technology or artifact is defined as bad or wrong, it is because it creates some kind of bad effect on the smooth operation of society. Things that used to be considered wrong can become right, and vice versa, depending on the situation. And the change has nothing to do with innate morality.

In modern society, this worldview is plainly seen in the various expressions of "political correctness" and in many of the ethical debates related to medicine and science. Naturalists see no ethical reasons why homosexuality cannot be normalized, euthanasia can't be practiced, human cloning can't be tried and embryonic stem cell research can't go forward.

Animism

The impact on culture, from Animism, is that there is no built-in inner drive to strive toward higher levels of achievement, either individually or as a society. The world, and life in general, are not moving toward a higher destination, so the tendency is simply to live life one day at a time and accept things the way they are. Anything "bad" that happens is seen to be the result of an offended spirit, so there is no compulsion to overcome an obstacle other than to find the offended deity and offer prayers and offerings. As a result, left to themselves, people in these cultures tend to remain in primitive circumstances with very little societal advancement. There is no compelling reason to seek progress. Where exceptions do occur, it is usually due to some other worldview being introduced that combines with the animistic one.

Far Eastern Thought

The primary impact of Far Eastern thought on culture is to promote passivism. In this worldview, nothing that we experience is a true expression of reality so there is no point in struggling to accomplish anything. The ultimate expression of it is to sit back and accept whatever happens and just allow the world to go by.

Theism

Theism has two primary outcomes as it relates to its impact on culture, depending on the type of theism being discussed. The first type basically lends itself to an impact on culture that is both moral and positive. It acknowledges both a spiritual and a physical part of reality which exists to fulfill a purpose, leads to a view of life that promotes meaning, establishes a specific "right" way to view morality and encourages a use of technology that promotes goodness. All the while, it is attempting to fulfill the purposes of God.

This category claims to receive direction from God, who is good and who directs his followers to be likewise. The instructions from God come in the form of some kind of revelation. But the God represented by this type of theism tends to operate impersonally in relationship to mankind. Mostly, God is acknowledged as existing, as creator, as all powerful, and as having given authoritative direction about how to live life, but he doesn't personally interact with individual humans on an intimate level.

The common result is a legalistic approach to living life and the development of culture. The moral order ought to be a certain way because it is written in the law or is put forth by "the prophet." It is, therefore, right to struggle against the moral wrongs in the world and change them to conform to the instructions given from God. And the way things ought to be are specifically prescribed.

The second form of Theism is represented by Relational Revelation. The end result of Relational Revelation on culture will be much the same as with the other forms of theism. It acknowledges both a spiritual and a physical part of reality which exists to fulfill a purpose, leads to a view of life that promotes meaning, establishes a specific "right" way to view morality and encourages a use of technology that promotes progress while attempting to fulfill the purposes of God.

It goes one step further, though. It does all of this in a way that puts a priority on a personal relationship with God as the motivation for fulfilling his purposes. Individuals try to create a moral culture because they love God, not simply because it is written in a book. We know what morality looks like because it is revealed in the revelation, but the reason for promoting it is love, not legalism. As a result, a culture is propelled toward goodness, selflessness, love and mercy, based on an inner drive rather than an outward command.

While the end result may look similar to that of other forms of theism, as it relates to the ultimate effect on culture, the mechanisms which bring it about are entirely different. Here it is not just the end result that matters. The means by which the outcome is brought about is also vital.

Every View Gets Expressed

While worldview largely exists behind the scenes, it is not a benign set of beliefs and values. Whether a person's worldview is conscious or unconscious, consistent or inconsistent, active or passive, theistic or atheistic, it is actively played out in life. Whatever worldview beliefs a person holds, becomes the guiding principles which shape what can and can't, what will and won't be done in daily life.

Now it is time to investigate one more aspect of worldview. Let's take a step back and examine more deeply the basic issues which relate to our ability to have confidence in our own worldview. Let's try and get an answer to the question, "Is there a way that we can honestly get at the truth?" In fact, there are some ways. Let's take a look.

Digging Deeper

1. As you consider the explanations above, what do you think about the end result of each of the worldviews?
2. Which of the results do you most identify with? Why?

The worst struggle I have ever had with my faith was in my college years, which I described previously. Since I reconciled that issue in my mind, I have been able to move forward in my faith life without that kind of doubt about God.

That being said, I still went many years without the confidence necessary to move forward with real assurance. I knew what I believed, but I was never sure how to put my beliefs up against someone else's and express how, and why, I was right and they were not. Not that I was wanting to put other people down, I just wanted to know why my own faith was the truth.

My study of worldview has moved me to that next level. It is not nearly so much an issue of being able to debate someone with a different set of beliefs. I can do it if I need to, but I don't really like it. Rather, it is a matter of having a settled belief and resolve that the way our human existence is described in the Bible is really the truth. In the past I knew it was true. Now I know why.

Understanding worldview will help you debate people with other belief systems if you want to do that. But more importantly, it will give you an understanding of the foundations of how we, as humans, perceive reality. With that solid foundation you will be able to move forward in your faith life with a peace and confidence you have never before known.

Chapter 7

Why We Lack
Confidence in Our Beliefs

Now faith is being sure of what we hope for and certain of what we do not see. Hebrews 11:1

Confidence in Our Beliefs

From the time I was a child, I have heard a piece of advice for getting along with people. That advice was, "Don't talk about religion or politics."

Why do you suppose that is so? I think it is because most people have strong beliefs about both of these things yet don't have strong confidence that they can defend them. As a result, people end up making statements that they can't intellectually back up, and conversations quickly degrade from a respectful intellectual exchange into an emotional tug of war.

I don't know about you, but over the last several years it seems to me that people are more and more willing to talk about these issues and take strong stands on them. The only problem is, the basis for the conversations still seem to primarily rest on an emotional foundation. I often hear people making bold statements about who they support politically or what they believe about war or sex or almost any other issue. But when pressed about why they believe the way they do, the response is something like, "That's just the way I believe."

Well, they have the right to respond that way if they want to. But it is a very poor foundation for living life, and certainly does not give a person any confidence to be bold in defending their beliefs.

I believe that every person has an obligation to him or herself to at least have a reasonable understanding as to why they have built their

45

lives on the foundation they have chosen. You can get away with a poor foundation for a while, but when a crisis hits, the life built on a poor foundation will crash.

Jesus told a parable about this very thing. He told the story about two men who each built a house. One built on a foundation of sand and the other on rock. When a really terrible storm hit, the house on the sand collapsed while the one on the rock stood firm.[1] Those houses are our lives and the foundations are our worldviews. We really need to know what we believe.

The Problem of Delusion

A number of years ago I knew a man who had some kind of mental disorder. He didn't go around with wild fiery eyes and didn't have spit drooling down his chin. He also was not a completely irrational person. In fact, if you just went up to him and began talking, you would find a very likable, engaging and, seemingly, normal person. You would never know that there was anything unusual about him at all.

But if you were to hang around him long enough, he would slowly begin changing the conversation to talk about the Bible and biblical truths. And if you were not aware of what he was doing, very soon you would be totally convinced that this guy was a tremendous biblical scholar. Of course, if you were up on what the Bible actually teaches, it wouldn't take you long to realize that a lot of the things he said were really kind of strange.

Here's what he would do. Whenever he would make a statement, he would give you Bible references to back up what he was saying. He would just throw out reference after reference after reference until a person had no choice but to affirm the "truth" of what he was saying. And the references he threw out were not just from a narrow portion of the Bible. He would grab things from everywhere.

The only problem was, he was making it all up. Believe me, he made it sound convincing! Anyone who did not know what was going on would be singularly impressed by his Bible knowledge and would never try to argue against him. But the really sad thing was, he really believed what he was saying. His delusion was an integral part of his personal reality.

But even with the strangeness of this situation, there is an interesting point that needs to be observed. This little delusion did not keep him from living his life pretty much the same as any other person. He held a job and participated in various social activities. It's just that his personal reality did not correspond completely with actual reality. Still, he was able to live his life one day after another just like everyone else. Of course there is one other observation that must also be recognized. As he continues to live out his life, there are things, such as various relationships or job opportunities, that will never quite work out right as long as his understanding of reality is skewed.

If we, as individuals, want to be able to effectively live out life and engage the world, we have to start with our understanding of the way that the world is structured. As with the young man above, it is actually possible for a person to live their entire life under a delusion. It is possible to make wrong assumptions, have strange values and beliefs and, in general, live a totally messed up life, but still negotiate life from birth till death. Many people, in fact, do just that. Some people intentionally operate their lives based on distorted beliefs as a way of getting what they want. Some do it because they never really examine the inconsistencies in their belief system. Still others end up this way as a result of a mental illness. All of these are a form of delusion.

It is not the ability to live life from beginning to end that is at issue when we deal with the topic of human experience. The real question we must deal with is, "Is there an actual, objective way that reality is organized and, if there is, can we know it?" If there is, and if we can, another important question follows: Am I willing to live my life according to that reality no matter where it leads, or am I willing to take the risk to live with the consequences of being out of sync with reality?

Deeper Issues

There are a lot of issues that people have varying opinions about these days. Many of the issues are of little consequence. People argue about which university has the highest quality education, which sports team is the best, which brand of coffee is the most flavorful or what is the most effective diet plan.

There are other issues, however, which relate to more than mere preference or opinion. They are issues that reflect a person's way of evaluating and living life. Based on these deeper issues, people actually create a lifestyle that guides the entire direction of their lives.

Most of these "life-affecting" issues are relatively non-controversial. They include such things as the value of having a job, getting an education or taking care of your children.

There are other issues, though, that have become real hot button issues such as homosexual marriage, pornography, profanity, lying, sexual activity outside of marriage, prejudice, bigotry, massive corporate profits, terrorism, obesity, drug and alcohol use, smoking, piracy, racism, pedophilia, prostitution, abortion, genocide, theft, and fraud, to name a few.

Most people look at that these hot-button issues and consider them immoral or evil. There are people, though, who will single out any one of these same issues and consider it to be a good thing, at least under certain circumstances. So, how should we approach our beliefs about these various topics? What is it that would make a person evaluate any one of them as either good or bad?

This brings us back, once again, to the proper way of evaluating human experience. An individual's judgment of what is good and bad depends on their understanding of the way the world actually operates. A person who believes that establishing and maintaining power is the highest value in life will interpret things one way. A person who strongly believes in looking out for the needs of others will see things differently. The person who believes there is no God will make one set of evaluations while the person who understands God to be a loving, personal individual will see things differently. The person who sees his own race or culture as superior will act one way while the person who considers all of mankind to be brothers will evaluate things a different way.

Hopefully you can now see how people can be deluded into believing something that is not true. Delusion doesn't mean that someone is mentally ill. Though that can be the root cause, most delusion is self-delusion as we make personal decisions not to actively pursue truth, or to actively pursue a worldview that is not truth.

But delusion is not the only problem that causes us not to have confidence in our worldview. Many people are simply confused and don't know where to look.

The Problem of Confusion

There are so many possible ways of evaluating human experience. And, to be sure, there are adherents of every conceivable view. But as we consider the possibilities we run into a very significant problem. Many of the viewpoints contradict one another. It is literally impossible for all of them to be right. So every person is out there doing all they can to discern how the world really works and how they can live life in a way that makes sense.

Now, whether or not we are able to personally figure out exactly how everything works is beside the point. The universe does exist in a particular, objective form. There is such a thing as truth—something that actually corresponds with the way our existence operates. Material and spiritual reality is structured in a particular way and not in other ways. The practical issues we have to deal with in our attempt to live life do not relate to whether or not there is such a thing as truth. Rather, it concerns the question, "Is it possible for us to individually sort it out in a way that allows us to match up our lives with actual reality?"

I do a certain amount of counseling, and I once had a young couple in my office who were having marital problems. In this particular case, it was initially rather difficult to get a handle on the real problem. It seemed that both of them had complaints against the other that related to truthfulness. They were both telling me different stories about the same events.

Since I had not known them before they came in, there was no way for me to know which one was telling the truth. They both sounded very convincing. Obviously, one was a very good liar. You can imagine how confusing that was for me and how difficult it is to help someone when you are not sure about the truth of what is going on.

But over a period of time I was able to get to know them a little better and began to see the truth for myself. As it turned out in this case, it was the husband who was the good liar. I believe he was so good because, at least in part, he believed his own lies. In spite of the fact that he had been abusive to his wife and kids and was an unfaithful marriage partner, in his own mind he was able to shift the blame to his wife. To him, his bad behavior was her fault so it was okay.

Until I knew the truth, I was struggling to figure out what kind of help to give. Before I was able to see what was really happening, all I could do was to give some general advice. But once I was able to see the true pattern of his actions, it didn't matter anymore what he said or how convincingly he said it. I knew the truth! Once I knew for sure where the problems were, I was able to be even more effective in helping with that situation.

Was I able to be of help to this couple before I knew the truth? I was to some extent—at least in the short term. But it wasn't until I understood the whole truth that the real solutions to their problems came into focus—until then I was confused.

Trying to figure out worldview is much like the situation with this couple. It is possible to be completely confused about worldview and still live life. In fact, literally millions of people do just that. They can do it because they are able to take the various components of their lives and deal with them in pieces.

Let's go back, for a moment, to the couple I was counseling. One of the things they told me was that they didn't take time out to communicate well. To deal with this I suggested a weekly date with just the two of them so they could make communication a more central part of their lives. It worked well for a while, but more talking was not a long-term solution. That was because, for this couple, poor communication was only a symptom of a deeper problem and not the problem itself. They were able to do specific activities which covered up the symptoms for a time, but eventually the real issues exposed themselves again.

That is what happens with people who live by false worldviews. They can find specific ways of thinking and acting that mask the inconsistencies in their lives for a time. When that quits working, they are able to make an adjustment and find some other activity to accomplish the same thing. It is possible for a person to do this throughout an entire lifetime and never come to grips with the truth.

The Key to Confidence

It may end up taking an individual quite some effort to come to an understanding of the way reality operates. But it is worth every bit of effort it takes. There is a worldview that is the truth—a way in which reality is actually organized. Those who are able to discover that truth and adjust their lives to live by it, will find a purpose and meaning in life that causes an unspeakable joy as all of life begins to make sense.

There is no way to look at any worldview and scientifically determine which one is right. There is too much that is simply beyond our ability to examine empirically. But there is a way to get at the truth by observing how each one matches up with the way the world actually operates—both physically and spiritually. If we can get a grip on that, our own confidence about how to live life will soar. Let's take a little time to explore how we can get at the truth.

Digging Deeper

1.   Do you have enough certainty in your beliefs that you can confidently talk with other people about them?
2.   If you don't, is your problem self-delusion or confusion?
3.   What can you do to move yourself past your limitations and have more confidence to stand firm in your beliefs?

Some people are content to live their lives on a foundation of uncertainty. Their approach is that if life issues are not decided firmly, they don't have to make a commitment to any particular moral standard. By living with uncertainty, they can console themselves with the fact that they really don't know what to do, so they don't have to take a chance of being wrong.

I do understand that feeling. After all, who likes to be proven wrong? But even though I understand the feeling, I cannot live my life based on that kind of uncertainty. I need resolution in my life. Without it I can't make progress and, to me, progress is more important than the discomfort I feel when I have to make a decision.

I am firmly convinced that God created me for a purpose, and to fulfill that purpose I have to discover what it is and act on it. God has given me the means to take that journey of discovery, and I am determined to give it everything I have.

Chapter 8

The Ultimate Basis for Choosing a Worldview

I tell you the truth, if you have faith as small as a mustard seed, you can say to this mountain, "Move from here to there" and it will move. Nothing will be impossible for you. Matthew 17:20

When I was a kid, I saw a plastic combination lock that you could see into. It was obviously not made to keep anything safe since you could easily break the plastic. What it was designed for was to give an education to people who were interested in observing how a combination lock works. As I turned the dial, I could see the gears and other mechanisms turn and move. This was a three-number lock, so you had to turn the dial to three specific, predetermined numbers to unlock it. When you followed the correct procedure, the locking mechanism moved out of the way so the lock would open.

The first turn was to the right. When I made that first turn, I could see three wheels turning around together. When I got to the correct number, the first wheel was positioned so that there was nothing to obstruct the locking mechanism.

The second turn was to the left. When I began this turn, the first wheel that was already in the right position did not move. But the second and third wheels turned left. When I got to the second correct number, the second wheel lined up with the first one so that neither was blocking the locking mechanism.

Finally, I turned the dial to the right, again. This time, only the third wheel moved. The other two stayed in the open position. When I got to the third correct number, all three wheels were lined up in a position, which didn't obstruct the locking mechanism, and I could pull it open.

Before I opened the lock, there were all kinds of unrelated things I could have done with it. I could have spun it on the table top, tossed it around, shoved it across the floor, turned the dials, studied it and so on. But until I had all three wheels lined up, I could not open it.

Our lives are much like a lock. We can do all kinds of things with them to mark time until we die. But until we get all of the wheels lined up by understanding the truth about life, we cannot unlock the secrets of meaning and purpose.

There are three wheels that must be lined up in order to get at the truth of worldview. These three wheels are faith, authority and evidence. Line them up in your life and the "truth will set you free."

Faith—The Foundation of Every Worldview

Suppose an alien spacecraft came and landed in your yard one night, and the aliens came into your house and abducted you. They wanted to find out a little more about humans so they took you into outer space on their spaceship and began performing experiments on your body. As a part of their experimentation, they inserted probes into your brain that were connected to a computer. By working in your brain with these probes, they were able to control which brain cells were being activated and could actually manipulate your thought processes and your memory.

To further develop their understanding, they took you back to your childhood and reconstructed your whole life from that point to the present. Then, to learn more about how the human brain works, they began to play with your thoughts and caused you to see things and experience events that had never happened.

After they had finally finished, they erased any memory you might have had of them, healed your wounds and gently put you back in your bed. Because of their manipulations, when you woke up the next morning you didn't remember being abducted. In fact, you didn't remember anything at all about their coming. You did remember, however, experiencing the events that they inserted into your brain during their experimentation. Until your dying day you would swear that those inserted "memories" were real, even though they had never really happened. In terms of your brain activity, the false experiences would be exactly the same as experiences you had really had in your life.

Now for the big question. How do you know that what was just described is not something that has actually happened to you? The answer is, you can't know! All you have to draw on is your subjective experience. There would be no objective way to separate the real from the unreal. In order to personally come to a conclusion about your memories, you have to go to the next level. You have to take a leap of faith and decide to believe that your senses are working correctly, and that the things you think you have experienced in your life were real experiences.

This is actually what we have to do every day in making judgments about every aspect of our existence. We see with our eyes, hear with our ears, and experience all kinds of other sensations with our senses. We have to trust that our brains are working properly and not feeding us delusions. And the only way we can really know that our memories are of real experiences, and not the manipulation of space aliens, is by faith. In that sense, faith is the whole foundation for every belief system. All worldviews are ultimately based on faith.

This truth is what makes talking about worldview so difficult. There is nothing based on physical observation or experiment that we can point to in any belief system and say this proves our system is right. It ultimately comes down to every person making a faith assumption that their personal beliefs are right. Faith is the spiritual organ that converts things not physically detected into personal certainty.

But don't get the wrong idea. This does not mean that it doesn't matter what you believe. Remember, we have already concluded that there is something that is actual reality. The questions we have to answer are, "What is that something?" and "How can we determine which way of believing is the right one?"

There really is a way that is real and there is a way to get at it. It's just that we can't find it based on physical observation and experimentation. We do, though, have evidence. We all perceive certain things about the structure of reality. We all see colors. We all experience gravity. We all interact with people in relationships. We all observe order in the universe. And we could go on and on listing the common things that humans experience as reality. What we have to do, then, is find the worldview that matches up most closely with the way we experience it.

For instance, there are groups which claim to be able to levitate their bodies into the air without the benefit of any kind of mechanical device. But the experience of virtually everyone in the world indicates that this belief is not consistent with reality. It is possible for people to adopt this kind of belief system if they want to, but it just isn't true. A worldview that wants to hang on to this kind of belief can be dismissed as not credible because it doesn't conform to the way human beings actually experience life.

Authority—Worldview Must Be Based on Something

There is something that is real. So how can we know what it is? Ultimately everyone grasps hold of something that they consider an authoritative explanation of the truth. There are several categories of authority.

Some groups look to some form of scripture—a revelation from God. The Christians have the Bible, the Muslims have the Koran, the Mormons have their Book of Mormon and we could go on and on with this.

There are other groups that depend on an oral tradition passed down through the ages. The Japanese Shinto religion depends on this approach along with most all of the pagan and animistic religions.

Then there are the groups that depend strictly on human reason. Numerous secular philosophies use this as their basis for authority. Most derivatives of naturalism such as nihilism, existentialism, secular humanism, postmodernism and positivism fall into this category. This is the "I can figure life out on my own" group.

Finally, we find groups that depend on "experience" as the basis for their authority. Many of the expressions of the New Age movement take this approach as well as some expressions of Far Eastern religions. Some groups look for their experiences by taking mind-altering drugs while others try to meditate their way to ultimate knowledge.

Regardless of what worldview a person holds, there is something that is considered the underlying authority that the view is based upon. The problem we run into, though, is that many of the worldviews, and by extension their associated authorities, contradict one another. They can't all be right. This leads us to take another step. There must be something that can help us figure out which authority can be depended upon.

Evidence—The Authority Has to be Believable

Aesop wrote a story about a shepherd boy who was out tending his sheep and got bored. He thought he would stir things up a bit, so he started shouting, "Wolf, wolf!" When the villagers heard him, they dropped everything they were doing to run where he was and kill the wolf. The only problem was, there was no wolf.

Well, the boy got the biggest charge out of seeing the villagers scramble like they did, so later, when he got bored again, he did the same thing. Of course, the villagers came running once more only to find that the boy was, again, not being truthful. His words did not match up with the reality of the situation.

Some time later, a real wolf came. The boy couldn't kill the wolf by himself, so he screamed to the villagers, "Wolf, wolf!" Only this time they didn't come. They didn't believe that he was telling the truth, and the wolf was able to ravage the flock.

There was a way that the villagers could have verified the truth of the situation. They actually took measures to verify the truth the first two times the boy screamed, "Wolf!" They went to where the flock was and analyzed the situation. Their analysis led them to conclude that reality was different than what the boy said.

The final time, when there really was a wolf, the villagers could have taken measures again to verify the truth, but this time they didn't. They simply went with their assumptions that the shepherd was lying again, and the sheep ended up being scattered and killed.

While we can't do physical experiments to verify the truth of any worldview, we can see how each one matches up with reality as we understand it. Each of the four types of authority can be analyzed and compared with what we do understand about reality.

We can read the scriptures of the various religions that claim an authority by revelation and see how they match up with what we know. Are they historically accurate? Are the characters believable? Does the teaching about God and reality match up with human experience?

For those which claim an oral tradition, we can ask the same kinds of questions. Does the mythology match up with history and experience? Does the world seem to operate the way the tradition expresses it?

Groups that depend on reason must also answer some tough questions. How can they be sure that their approach is right and all others are wrong? How do they account for the things that can't be explained based on their philosophy?

Finally, those who depend on experience must account for experience that is different from their own. They must answer why their experience is right and contradictory experiences are not right.

Which Worldview Best Meets the Standard?

It is impossible, in this book, to go into great detail about each worldview. There are plenty of people who have done just that and you will find information in the "resources" section of the appendix where you can do deeper research into this topic.

Since that is not the focus of this work, we will not delve deeply into this topic, here. However, in order to at least get a sense of the big picture, we will take just a moment to summarize the issues that each basic worldview category struggles with.

Naturalism

The primary authority that Naturalism uses is reason. The big problem with naturalism's use of this authority, though, is that it is unable to even consider that there may be more to reality than just the material world. It has no objective basis for its foundational belief (that matter is all that exists)—it just assumes it. It doesn't recognize that there may be other forms of evidence for aspects of reality that cannot be accessed by observation and experiment.

Even the physical evidence which points to something beyond the natural (of which there is plenty) cannot be evaluated completely, because the category necessary for evaluating it is not acknowledged. It has no way to explore, or even talk about, the possibility that there might be a "spiritual" reality beyond the "natural."

Animism

The primary source of authority for Animism is oral tradition. The problem with this understanding of reality is that it plays down one of the most important, and obvious, elements of humanity—the ability to grow and learn. Societies which do emphasize research and development are able to progress socially, politically, economically and in many other ways that do not make sense under Animism. Large doses of dynamic creativity simply don't exist in animistic societies.

Far Eastern Thought

Far Eastern thought tends to use experience as its primary source of authority, though different groups do have their scriptures, as well. It is virtually impossible to function practically and consistently under this worldview. It creates a situation where people are forced to live by values and behaviors that they, themselves, acknowledge to be meaningless. The attempt to be creative, to grow, to invent, to find meaning and to seek freedom are all central elements of human experience. Yet all of these things directly contradict the supposed reality of Far Eastern thought. Even people who sincerely believe it cannot consistently live by it.

Theism (Non-relational)

The primary source of authority for most theistic groups is some book that they consider to be a revelation from God. In this approach to reality we run into much the same problem that we have run into with the other worldviews. This way of thinking nullifies one of the key elements of human experience. By relegating God to a non-personal being, it lowers mankind to that level as well. Rather than putting an emphasis on relationship, which we were obviously designed for, the emphasis for life shifts to the accomplishment of activities and the fulfillment of duties. We are certainly capable of that, and the emphasis is good as far as it goes. But the ultimate expression of human experience is only found in relationship.

Relational Revelation

The authority for Relational Revelation is the Bible (both Old and New Testaments). This is the understanding of reality that lines up most closely with how humans experience life. It takes seriously both physical and spiritual reality and emphasizes relationship, while not discounting human activity.

Taking the Next Step

As we move on through the rest of this book, Relational Revelation will be dealt with more fully. From here we will try and get a grasp on how a better understanding of worldview can help us deepen our faith, strengthen our relationship with God and become more effective in generating a greater good in the world.

At this point we are going to begin to focus more deeply on the implications of Relational Revelation. If it really is the "truth," then it is important to understand the nature of it and what a worldview based on it would produce in life.

Relational Revelation describes reality in terms of the Kingdom of God. We will now take some time to explore the meaning of that concept.

Digging Deeper

1. What parts of your belief system are strictly faith statements?
2. To what extent do you rely on revelation, oral tradition, experience and human reason as the authority for what you believe? Which one is primary?

3. How solid is the evidence for the reliability of your primary authority?

What do you think about when you hear the phrase, "Kingdom of God"? Is it some abstract spiritual idea that is important as a theological concept, but doesn't really have any direct implications for your life? That's the way I used to think about it. For me, I think there were two problems.

First, I didn't have a real concept of a kingdom. I have never lived in one, and the ones I have seen in operation have been either movie depictions (more like fantasy) or the ceremonial functions performed by foreign royalty who don't have any real political power.

The second problem relates to the fact that I can't physically experience God's Kingdom. As a result, it has been hard for me to understand how that directly impacted my daily life.

I have, though, finally come to a new level of understanding about the reality of the Kingdom. I have come to recognize that the spiritual laws that God has established are objective realities (even if spiritual) and that they are right and true. I see that living by them leads to life and purpose, while ignoring them leads to meaninglessness and death.

The personal grasp and acceptance of the fact that I am a citizen of a real and eternal kingdom has transformed my life. I can now make living by the principles of God's Kingdom my highest allegiance.

Chapter 9

Ultimate Reality—
The Culture of the Kingdom

Once, having been asked by the Pharisees when the kingdom of God would come, Jesus replied, "The kingdom of God does not come with your careful observation, nor will people say, 'Here it is,' or 'There it is,' because the kingdom of God is within you." Luke 17:20-21

What Is a Kingdom?

What form of government will you find in England? How about Japan? The most obvious answer is that they are parliamentary democracies. They both have parliaments which make laws, and the representatives who serve in those parliaments are elected by the people. But both of them also have a monarch. England has its king or queen, and Japan has its emperor.

Of course, in modern times, these monarchs primarily perform a ceremonial function. There is a government connection, but it is more like a "rubber stamp" role than a decision making one. There was a time, though, when the monarchy, in both of these countries, had absolute political power. There was none of this "power in the hands of the people" stuff.

The first thing we need to grasp, if we are going to really understand the Kingdom of God and the culture associated with it, is the concept of kingdom. There are still a few small kingdoms around the globe, but in the modern world not too many people still live in an honest to goodness kingdom.

Even though there are a number of countries which still have a monarchy, most of them have moved beyond having a king or queen who actually rules the country. Like the two mentioned above, modern monarchies tend to be more ceremonial. They stand as symbols for their countries. The monarchs themselves may interact with the politicians and diplomats of other countries in order to promote the political and economic interests of their state, but they don't make laws and enforce them. They don't run the government.

In a real kingdom, though, the monarch is not a symbol. The highest member of the royal family is actually the head of state. That person is the absolute ruler and is responsible for running the government and for making and enforcing laws. And when cases are brought to trial the monarch is the final judge and jury. The monarch also runs the diplomatic corps and makes all final decisions related to foreign policy. What he or she says is the final word in all affairs of state. If you don't like it, you can't vote him or her out. You better learn to live with it or leave!

This does not mean, necessarily, that the monarch is a tyrant. In fact, there have certainly been some very benevolent rulers throughout history. But the point is, a real king or queen has the power to run the kingdom however they want.

What Is the Kingdom of God?

The Kingdom of God represents the ultimate expression of reality. It is the place where God is the king in the most unequivocal sense of the word! He is the absolute ruler. He establishes the order, makes the rules, then enforces them. This is not meant to imply, in any way, that it is a place of oppression, or anything else negative. In fact, God is the most benevolent ruler that can possibly be imagined.

In some ways, though, the image of king is not an adequate description of God. In this case we are trying to describe a spiritual concept using physical terminology. God's rulership goes well beyond anything we can experience from any earthly ruler.

First of all, he did not simply take over a kingdom by succeeding a parent or by staging a coup. God actually created, from scratch, the things he wanted, and organized them to be the way they are. He established the workings of the spiritual order. He created material reality out of nothing from his own imagination.[1] He invented, and put in place, the laws of the physical universe. He created living beings of all kinds and created mankind after his own image as a special part of that creation. Not only did he create it, he is responsible for keeping it going according to his own purposes.[2] He is the owner and operator of it all. Nothing would exist without his creative efforts and nothing would continue without his active intervention.

This is much more than a kingdom but, in our limited earth experience and vocabulary, we don't have a better way of expressing the concept. So we express the operation of God's creation as a kingdom with him as the absolute monarch. Things were begun according to his desires; the world operates according to those same desires and will ultimately end in accordance with his purposes.[3]

What Is the Nature of the Kingdom Culture?

We have already seen that every societal grouping somehow expresses itself in the form of a culture. The Kingdom of God is no exception. But since this is a spiritual kingdom, the questions related to culture are focused a little differently than with material cultures. The culture of the Kingdom of God is certainly able to be expressed in material reality, and faithful Kingdom citizens will live out Kingdom values in their physical lives. But the essence of the culture itself is not physical.[4] There you will not find eating utensils and electronic technologies. This kingdom is spiritual, and the expressions of it are primarily spiritual and moral. They are expressed in material reality as they overlay the various physical cultures in our material world.

Any technology and artifacts that may exist in God's spiritual reality are outside of our ability to interact with. We are limited to working strictly within the material universe. So when we, as material human beings, begin to deal with our place in the Kingdom of God, it is not the technology and artifact issues we deal with, it is strictly the nonmaterial aspects of the culture.

God's Role in the Kingdom

We have already touched on some of the things that relate to God's activity in the operation of the Kingdom, and there is no need to rehash everything that has already been said. It is important for us to make the point, though, that God does establish the rules and plays an active role in the operation of his kingdom.

Our tendency, as human beings, is to place ourselves at the center of our universe. Because of our human nature, we do have the ability to mentally conceive of an existence where we are the center. But that is not reality! God is the center, and his will and purpose are the ruling forces. He created everything, and he keeps it going. He has a purpose in it and all of history is moving toward the ultimate fulfillment of that purpose. In other words, everything is about God, not about us! Think what we may, the ultimate outcome of history will be what God directs it to be, not what we want it to be.[5]

Mankind's Role in the Kingdom

Ultimately things will play out the way God decides they will play out. Mankind has no place, whatsoever, in deciding the ultimate direction of things. We were created to fulfill a purpose that God decided, and that purpose will be accomplished no matter what we do.

But that does not mean that we, as individual humans, don't matter. In fact, mankind plays a central role in the purpose of God that is utterly profound. God created us special so that he would have a race of people with whom he could personally interact throughout the rest of eternity.[6]

God is a social being and has a need for personal interaction with like beings. But there is only one being like God. So he created mankind in his own image. This image is not a physical likeness. Rather, it is a spiritual likeness.[7] It is impossible to know the full extent of what this means, but human beings have many of the characteristics of God himself, only to a lesser degree. These characteristics include such things as spirit, knowledge, creativity, personality, gender, eternalness, dominion, free will and self-consciousness.

As we carefully examine these characteristics, a marvelous thing becomes evident. These attributes allow us to operate in the realm where God himself dwells. If a person has characteristics like the ones above, he is able to choose for himself how he will live. He can even choose whether or not to have God around.

So God created a proving ground—material reality. Certainly our material world is more than a mere proving ground, but that is certainly an important part of the mix. This proving ground is a place where these new spiritual creations are able to live out life. Here, in this place, we are able to decide whether we want to live out the rest of eternity in relationship with God, or not. It is God's hope, and intention, that all would choose his path, but ultimately each individual has to make that choice.[8]

God could have created robots who would all worship and adore him, but that is not the kind of relationship he wants. He wants a loving relationship with beings who fully and freely love him—just because they want to. Those who make the choice to love God that way will have the opportunity to be in that relationship with him throughout the rest of eternity. Those who don't want it are deliberately making the choice to live their eternity outside of his presence.[9] Mankind's role in the kingdom is to live in relationship with God and express their love to him directly by the way they live life in the material world.

How the Kingdom Is Ordered

Kingdom culture has its own distinct way of ordering life and it is all based on the character of God, himself. God is love,[10] so the Kingdom is designed to provide the opportunity for love to be expressed unreservedly. God is holy,[11] so the Kingdom is designed in a way that precludes any evil from even entering its boundaries. God is righteous,[12] so the Kingdom is designed so that everything that happens is right and just.

It doesn't take a rocket scientist to realize that this kind of existence does not reside completely in any material culture. Every culture on earth has its share of hate, impurity and injustice. The qualities of the Kingdom culture only exist in their ultimate form in the Kingdom itself. While the supreme expression of Kingdom culture only exists in that part of spiritual reality where God dwells, there is a place on earth where an outward expression also exists, even if imperfectly. That place is in the hearts of those who have chosen a relationship with him.[13]

A person who is part of American culture can't express unreserved love, but Americans who have the Kingdom of God in their hearts can. A South African citizen can't be absolutely holy, but a person who is a citizen of South Africa, and who has the Kingdom of God in his heart, has the ability to express that kind of purity in life. A Cambodian citizen can't be perfectly righteous, but a Cambodian who is a citizen of the Kingdom can live righteousness out in life. To be sure, no person who lives in the material world has the ability to do these things perfectly. The corrupted part of our human existence keeps getting in the way. But the seed, the power and the potential are all there. It is possible for us to develop our lives so that the Kingdom qualities are more and more evident as we conform ourselves to Kingdom culture.

How the Kingdom Is Expressed in the Material Universe

In the interaction of cultural groups on earth, when one culture intersects another, there are several possible things that can happen. No particular one of these is inevitable, but there will be some kind of result.

One possibility is that one of the cultures will swallow up the other. The person who enters a different culture and is completely taken by it, may choose to throw away his mother culture and adopt the new one. This is an extreme but, while it does happen, it is not the norm.

Another possibility is the opposite scenario. Here, a person enters a different culture and is so repulsed by it that he rejects it completely and refuses to adopt any aspect of it. This is also an extreme. And while this one may be more common than the first, it is still not the norm.

The most common outcome is that a few of the cultural elements from one culture are appreciated and incorporated into the other. This may involve such things as art appreciation, vocabulary, values, ways of looking at life, the technology that is used in daily life, food and so on. In my own life, from time to time, I still use chopsticks to eat rice—something I adopted from my life in Japan. The range of what might be adopted is very wide. In some cases it may involve just a couple of items. In others, one culture may end up having a very large influence on another.

What is true concerning material culture is also true regarding Kingdom culture. In societies that have a long Christian tradition, the influence of Kingdom culture can be seen in such matters as the law, the view of technology, how sexuality is understood, how life is valued and many other things. This does not mean that all of the people in the culture are Christians. Far from it! It is just that the influence of Kingdom culture, at some point in history, was so strong that it generated a way of thinking and acting that has filtered down into many facets of the society throughout many generations.

On the other side, there are cultures in the world which contain a lot of darkness and evil—cultures which have had little or no influence from Kingdom culture. In these cultures, things such as homosexuality, abortion, prostitution, drug use, adultery and even murder may not be seen as completely unacceptable behavior.

No matter which side a material culture tends toward, there will be issues that need the enlightenment of the Kingdom. There is no material culture that is completely bad, but there are also none which are totally aligned with the Kingdom. Kingdom culture exists in an entirely different dimension from every material culture. When someone is faced with the idea of becoming a member of the Kingdom, they have a decision to make.

One possible decision is to try and accept Kingdom culture so fully that they completely throw out material culture. Some have become hermits and monks in an attempt to do this. But ultimately it is impossible as long as a person still lives in the material world.

Another possibility is to totally reject the Kingdom. Many people do this, as well. They decide that they don't want anything to do with God and his ways.

As in the situation with material culture, there is a third option. That third way is somewhere in between. The possibilities range all the way from expressions of massive good to those of massive evil. The best case is for a large majority of the people in a culture to adopt completely the values and ways of the Kingdom, and for its citizens to live life in their material culture in a way that causes it to be made better. Under this scenario, all forms of sexual activity outside of marriage would be considered wrong, not accepting personal responsibility for one's actions would be looked down upon, people would go out of their way to help their fellow man, and so on.

Let's look at an example of how the values of Kingdom culture might affect a culture in our world. If a material culture was one which worshiped many gods, one of the most obvious ways Kingdom culture would cause change would relate to the whole idea of how to worship God. The Kingdom value of "one God" would certainly have a huge impact on worship forms.

The concept of love also has a different meaning for polytheistic cultures than it does in the Kingdom. If the Kingdom value of love were overlaid on a culture which worshiped many gods, you might see a profound effect on the way that men and women view and treat each other or the way that a father interacts with his son.

Of course, to fully impact another culture with Kingdom values, a person would have to introduce the culture to a personal relationship with God through Jesus Christ, as well as to the biblical concepts of love, mercy, grace, redemption, holiness and justice. The more of these values that are overlaid on any material culture the more changes will take place within it. But this is not something that destroys the earthly culture. Rather, it helps to complete it.

If the particular matters that make a culture unique are evil—things like wife beating, human sacrifice, wanton sexual immorality, torture, and the like—then those aspects of the culture need to be changed. There is no value in uniqueness when a cultural trait is evil. But there is no compelling reason why most cultural elements that relate to uniqueness cannot be maintained. Arabs can still wear their native dress, Chinese can still use their chopsticks, bikers can still drive their Harleys, cowboys can still wear their boots and the Japanese can still eat their sushi.

Relational Revelation is the worldview that represents the

Kingdom of God. It is the standard by which the spiritual and moral elements of every material culture must be measured. The values expressed in it are the Kingdom's values and are able to overlay any and every material culture. To the degree it is accomplished a culture will be completed, not diminished.

Digging Deeper

1.   When you think of God as the king, what does that imply regarding your relationship to him?

2.   To what degree have you adopted Kingdom culture as your own?

3.   How does your acceptance of Kingdom culture affect the way you interact with material culture?

I have spent a good deal of time thinking about the process of making choices. I have come to the conclusion that there are two levels of choices.

The first level is rather shallow. It involves things like selecting which brand of cereal you will buy in the grocery store, or what soft drink you will take from the cooler at the picnic. You make these kinds of choices dozens of times per day, but typically the results of these don't have any significant impact on your life.

There is another level of choice, though, that is significant. These choices are actually decisions that move your entire life in a particular direction. They might include such things as what profession to pursue or whom to marry.

The most profound decision I have ever made in my life was to enter into a personal relationship with God through Jesus Christ. It has not only affected my eternal destiny, but has had a profound impact on my language, personal morality, relationships and many other things.

I have had the opportunity to share my faith in Christ with many people, and it has been a real schooling to watch those interactions. When I have an opportunity to share my faith with others, I watch as they choose to follow Christ or to reject him. In any given circumstance the final outcome will be one or the other.

As I watch them make the decision, it is almost invariably a very emotional choice. It is emotional because it is a worldview choice. Whatever they choose changes the direction of their life in a conscious and profound way.

Chapter 10

Choosing a Worldview for Yourself

This is love for God: to obey his commands. And his commands are not burdensome, for everyone born of God overcomes the world. This is the victory that has overcome the world, even our faith. Who is it that overcomes the world? Only he who believes that Jesus is the Son of God. 1 John 5:3-5

The Nature of Choice

Let me admit up front, that this chapter expresses my take on the nature of making a choice. I recognize that there are other opposing views. This is the one that makes the most sense to me.

That being said, the reason there are different ways of looking at this issue is that there is some confusion about how to interpret certain segments in the documents that people use as their worldview authority. My view emerges out of a particular way of interpreting biblical passages on the topic of choice. Some people have a different take on this as it relates to their own conversion experience.

Before going any further, I want to make one special point. There is a line of belief that a person cannot cross and still be considered a Christian. Once that line is crossed, a person has moved over to a different worldview—one that is not Christian. But there are some issues that Christians disagree about that do not cross that line. We can honestly disagree on some things and still be counted among the citizens of the Kingdom. A person's understanding about choice is one of those areas. It may affect how we go about worshiping and expressing our faith, but does not affect whether or not we are children of the King. Now, with that disclaimer out of the way, let's look at choice.

A winning mentality is an interesting phenomenon. I like sports and watch sporting events whenever I have the opportunity. Like most people, I especially enjoy watching winners. Sometimes, selecting which team will be a winner is an obvious choice. Winning teams tend to be the ones with superior athletes, superior coaching and teammates who manage to work together well.

But sometimes you look at a particular team and wonder what it is that causes them to keep winning. There are no unusual standouts, but they always seem to find a way to win.

This kind of mentality is such an intangible that it is almost impossible to completely identify. But underneath all of the intangibles you will always find one thing—an expectation that they will win. In fact, they expect it to the point that if they lose, they are totally surprised. They don't understand how it could even happen. This kind of group is so committed to winning that they will do whatever it takes to overcome the obstacles. They make a choice to completely throw themselves, body and soul, into making sure that the outcome is victory.

If you look only at talent, you will never be able to select the winners. Every professional team, of every sport, is filled with superior talent. The athletes would not have made it to that level if it were not so.

However, even among superior athletes there is a hierarchy of talent. Some are stars while others are superstars. Yet some people with superstar talent don't make it to the top while others, with average star talent, manage to crawl to elite status. The difference is in the choices they make to continue improving. The average person with great heart will ultimately win out over the superior talent with no heart. Everything ultimately depends on the choices they make about how far they are willing to progress.

This principle does not just apply to athletes. It applies to every person in every area of life. We choose how good we will be on the job, in the family and in our relationship with God.

The Mechanism of Choice

When it comes to our decision to enter into a relationship with God, sometimes it may seem outwardly that God just sort of sneaks up and "jumps" people to convert them. But he doesn't! Something first has to happen in the heart of an individual. A person has to open his or her heart to God by an act of the will.[1]

This does not, necessarily, mean that the opening was a carefully thought out decision. I have had many experiences in my faith life when God made himself known to me in a very emotional and dramatic fashion without my having thought deeply about it in advance. My own decision to receive Christ into my life was like that.

But these experiences don't just happen. We have to put ourselves into a position where we allow it. God knows the exact moment of that opening, and he sometimes reveals himself personally at that precise instant. For some, the experience happens so quickly, and is so profound, that it seems like there was no willful action taken at all. But God never violates our will. This does not mean that he has given up his sovereignty. Ultimately the direction of history and the fate of the world still lie in his hands.

Here's how that happens. The Bible tells us that when God stepped out of heaven to become the man Jesus Christ, he had to limit himself to the confines of material reality. He could not bring all of the glories of heaven with him to earth. Material reality cannot hold it.[2]

When it comes to our human ability to make choices, God again had to limit himself in order to allow us the possibility of a free will. In the broad sense, he is still able to override human choice to accomplish his ultimate purpose in history. Only he has stepped back to allow both the human determination of their own individual fate and the implications of those choices to play out in the world. God has made it abundantly clear that his will is for every individual human to enter into his Kingdom as a citizen.[3] It is also clear that not everyone does.[4]

The Bible is full of examples, and of language, that teach this truth. Beginning at the very beginning, God didn't want Adam and Eve to disobey, but they did.[5] And God didn't create the human race for the purpose of destroying them in the flood so he could start over. It was the choice of the people to reject God that resulted in their judgment.⁶ Then, what about the nation of Israel? Throughout the en-tire recorded history of the Old Testament, God was calling the nation to be faithful to him. God was not controlling them and causing them to move from faithfulness to unfaithfulness then back again. When they chose to be faithful, he took care of them. When they rebelled, he sent judgment.⁷

We see the same teaching in the New Testament. Jesus was always pressing people to choose to follow him and was always disappointed when they did not. The rich young ruler refused.⁸ Matthew⁹, Peter¹⁰ and Zacchaeus¹¹ took him up.

Additionally, the writers of the New Testament were constantly urging people to follow God and warning them of the consequences of not doing so.¹² Paul spent a great portion of all of his letters telling people the choices they should be making—from the need to person-ally enter into a relationship with Christ, to proper conduct among be-lievers, to the ethical choices of daily living. These "callings" are all invitations. People choose, on their own, to accept them or not.

Besides the examples in Scripture, almost every one of us can identify times in our lives when we have accepted the calling and times when we have rejected it. We have also seen this played out in the lives of others.

The mechanism of choice is to face a worldview and to make a de-cision—for or against. The degree to which we were conscious of that decision is not the issue. The point is, a decision is made. When that decision is made, a change in attitude and lifestyle occurs.

An individual's worldview is not what he or she says it is, it is what actually plays out in life. When a person is committed to a worldview, whether it came from a conscious or a subconscious choice, that person will live in a way that fulfills the values of that system. You cannot understand your worldview by writing down what you think you believe. You find out about it by analyzing what you do. It is pos-sible for a person to change the worldview he lives by, but along with that comes a profound life change.

The Scope of Choice

One more thing should also be said about our decision to accept God. There is an initial change that takes place in which we choose to exit our previous worldview and enter the Kingdom of God. But there are also degrees to which we allow that change to develop. It is God's intention that, when we enter into relationship with him, we give ourselves fully to everything that entails. Some people experience the change but never even try to understand how it is supposed to impact the rest of life. Certainly some of the things regarding their understanding about God change. But the way they live their lives stays pretty much the same.

So, in one sense, we should constantly be deciding to make changes in our lives. Not that we keep leaving and reentering a relationship with God, but our understanding of the implications of Kingdom life continues to grow and expand throughout life. Every time we recognize an area of life where we are not in alignment with God's revealed will, we should be actively seeking to accept God's direction and implement the change. Ultimately it all happens as we confront our own worldview decisions and choose what direction we will go.

It is my belief that Relational Revelation is the most logical of all worldviews. I believe that anyone who honestly examines the various possibilities, and takes them to their logical conclusions, must come to the determination that Relational Revelation is the only one worthy to be followed. I believe that the primary reason people refuse to accept this worldview is because they are not willing to submit themselves to the demands (intellectual and moral) of the God of the Bible. In that case, they must find some other belief system and ignore the inconsistencies.

The Most Radical Choice— Changing Worldviews

When I lived in Latvia, I hosted a radio show called *Freddy and Friends*. On this show I played Christian music and usually brought on a guest to interview. During the show's run, I probably interviewed close to 100 people. Quite often my guests were missionaries from the various groups and denominations who were working in the country. As I talked with the different guests, I would ask them about their own story of how they decided to become a Christian—their conversion experience.

The experiences were quite varied. Some saw their entry into the Kingdom as a highly charged emotional experience. Some just grew up from childhood in their faith and virtually never questioned it. Some entered faith through a thoughtful search for truth. Some spoke in tongues, and some didn't.

The interesting thing, though, is that the type of group the individuals were affiliated with tended to be closely related to the way they experienced their change. The experience of many of the interviewees was quite different from the way I experienced my own worldview change. Some of their "nonessential" theological beliefs were different from my own. But the one thing that was evident in every one was a strong personal commitment to a relationship with Jesus Christ.

Maybe some of us are just wrong about our ideas of what creates this change. More likely, there is simply more than one way that people experience it—not more than one way that it actually happens.

But it is not our particular experience of change that is so critical, it is the fact that it actually happens. Those who do experience it, regardless of the specific nature of the experience, enter into relationship with God. Those who don't are separated from him.

I believe that most of the time, when this kind of change takes place in an individual's life, it is not the result of a thoughtful process, though some people do experience it that way. It usually happens when a person hears an explanation of the worldview of the Kingdom, or experiences some kind of interaction with the worldview, and it just all of a sudden makes sense. At that point they simply recognize it as the truth or as the touch of God and make a choice to follow it.

Most commonly, though not always, the sensation that accompanies the choice is one of profound emotion. But regardless of the feelings, all who have the experience tend to move forward in life, from that time on, in a fashion that is consistent with how they perceived the conversion. Let's go one step further, now and see how this level of choice operates.

Digging Deeper

1.   If you have already done so, when did you make the choice to enter into a personal relationship with God?
2.   How did you experience that choice? Was it emotional? Rational?
3.   How has your experience been played out in your life?
4.   What kinds of choices do you make on a daily basis as a result of your choice to follow God?

When I was sixteen years old, I had an encounter with God that changed my life. Actually, many people might be surprised at the radical nature of the change. Before my change, I was not a "bad" kid. I never drank alcohol or did drugs, was not sexually active, made good grades and played sports. I was certainly not perfect, but was basically a good kid.

The change I experienced was an internal change. When I met God, my life took on a meaning that I had never before known. All of a sudden, I had a reason for acting good that I didn't have before. I wanted to make a difference in the lives of other people and to share how God had changed my life.

My change was different from people who had stepped out of drug addiction or Satan worship. I didn't have to stop participating in all kinds of activities that society frowns upon, so outwardly my transformation may not have seemed dramatic. But for me it was like stepping out of a black and white world into technicolor. The change was radical and influenced the entire direction of my life.

Chapter 11

The Choice That Changes the World

Jesus answered, "I tell you the truth, no one can enter the kingdom of God unless he is born of water and the Spirit. Flesh gives birth to flesh, but the Spirit gives birth to spirit. You should not be surprised at my saying, 'You must be born again.'" John 3:5-7

The transformation that takes place when a caterpillar becomes a butterfly is truly amazing. It changes from an ugly, heavy, many legged, earth bound, long, crawly thing to a colorful, elegant, light, winged creature with fewer legs and the ability to fly. Someone who didn't know that butterflies come from caterpillars would, absolutely, never guess because they are so radically different.

In our material world, these kinds of changes happen in various places. A maggot turns into a fly; an egg the size of a pinhead turns into a fish.

But the most remarkable transformations that I have ever witnessed happen when people change from being devilishly evil to purposeful, productive citizens. I have heard many testimonials from people who grew up in and out of the hands of the law, dealing and using drugs, engaging in prostitution or beating up people. These people eventually changed to become accountants, social workers, preachers and the like. This kind of transformation only happens when there is a radical shift in worldview.

The Ultimate Choice

In Christian circles there is a word we use when we talk about a change of worldview—"conversion." This is the term we use to speak of the choice which causes a transformation in one's belief system. It is the shift that a person makes when stepping from unbelief to belief in Christ.

But, in order not to get ourselves confused, we need to recognize that this word is used in other contexts, as well. For instance, we sometimes refer to a person converting from one denomination to another or from one political party to another. Sometimes we even use the word to describe a decision that doesn't have a profound impact on a person's life at all—like switching loyalty from one brand of cola to another. But the true sense of the word indicates a seismic shift in the underlying foundation of a person's life that causes them to think and to live life differently than they did before.

When a person meets Christ in a personal encounter, this kind of shift occurs. But conversion is not limited to changing from non-Christian to Christian. People who grew up under a Christian belief system sometimes have this kind of shift and become naturalists (atheists), Buddhists or even followers of a modern cult. You yourself may have experienced a shift like this as a result of a college course which shook your belief system, a divorce, the death of someone you loved deeply, a war or even the events of 9/11/2001. We need to get a handle on this phenomenon because, if we want to join the battle and be involved in winning the worldview war, we have to operate on a level where conversion happens.

What is this conversion thing, anyway? Simply put, conversion is a shift, or change, in the way that you think about life. It causes you to see the world, and to act, in ways that are different than you did before. To use a theme from earlier in the book, it is a change in the lens that you use to understand reality.

What we are particularly interested in is the conversion that happens when a person enters into a relationship with God. In this arena, conversion is not a psychological, emotional or mental shift, though psychological, emotional or mental shifts often happen when a person actually meets God. Conversion is something that God does to us after we make a deliberate decision to allow it to happen.[13] It is, in effect, a partnership between God and man, where an individual allows the change and God creates it. It is the change that is described in 2 Corinthians 5:17 where Paul writes, "Therefore, if anyone is in Christ, he is a new creation; the old has gone, the new has come!"

It is one thing to know what needs to be done; it is another thing altogether to actually do it. It is entirely possible for a person to know what is right, but never take the step to open the heart to God and allow him to create the change.

If we want to influence our culture toward the Kingdom of God, two things have to happen. First, we have to individually become a person whose life has been converted to the point that we unreservedly join the battle. Second, we have to put our whole being into an effort to encourage the conversion of others. We intuitively know this needs to happen, but what can we do to move it along?

Most people actually resist conversion in any form, particularly as it relates to joining the family of God. But if we want to see a change in culture, we need to take on a different attitude. If we know the truth, doesn't it make sense to actually seek out the changes necessary to make that a part of our lives, rather than run from them? It certainly makes sense, but it is far from everyday reality.

There are two places where we need to become active in promoting this kind of conversion. The first is in our own lives. But once we have personally made that step, we need to work toward a second one. We need to be active in leading others to take the step, as well. Let's look at those two places and see how they play out in life.

Conversion in Ourselves

You may be reading this and wonder why you need your own conversion. You may be thinking, "This has already happened to me." Well, maybe it has or maybe it hasn't. Your first order of business is to make sure. And how do you know? You know by the way you live. Do you spend time personally interacting with God? Is your life holy as the Bible defines holiness? Do you know God's calling on your life and are you actively pursuing it? Is the Kingdom of God expanding and being strengthened by the way you engage the various relationships in your life?

There are three possibilities as you consider your own life. The first is that you definitely do live a life that is in line with God's revelation (not that you have achieved perfection, but you are actively and intentionally working toward that goal). The second possibility is the opposite extreme—that you definitely do not have a biblical world-view. The final possibility is that you believe the biblical view is the right one, but you only partially live by it.

If your life pattern is characterized by either of the last two possibilities, you need a personal conversion in order to completely conform yourself to the ways of God. There are two steps that you will have to take in order to change your worldview from what it currently is to what it needs to be.

The first step is to immerse yourself in the truth. By that is meant that you must get to the place where you accept the elements of God's Kingdom in your heart of hearts. This involves coming to a point in your life where you are able to answer the seven worldview questions in a way that is consistent with what is taught in the Bible.

For instance, the first worldview question is, "What is the nature of ultimate reality?" If you answer that it is the God of the Bible, you must go beyond intellectually knowing that God is holy, just, loving, merciful and so on. You must also understand how these characteristics of ultimate reality affect you personally. You have to understand that the holiness of God is also a requirement for your life and be willing to put aside thoughts and activities that don't express it. It is not enough to know intellectually that God is personal. You have to get to the place where you actually interact personally with God. You need to go through this kind of process with all of the worldview questions. You must come to the place in your life where you answer them according to the way God's revelation expresses them.

But there is a second step that must be made. The final step of conversion is to make a deeply personal decision that you are going to actually live by the worldview. It is at this point that trying to understand and implement the process becomes really difficult. This is the place where people often believe the worldview with their minds, but only live it out inconsistently. It can't simply be a surface level decision. It is a decision to give yourself, heart and soul, to God—not to the worldview, but personally to God! You come to the place in your life where God is so real and personal to you that you see the world through his eyes and you constantly experience his presence.

Conversion in Others

There is a second place where we have to become active in working toward conversion, and that relates to our mission in the Kingdom of God. It is possible for us, as individuals, to take the initiative toward our own conversion as we consider the things that are not right in our lives and willfully move in the direction of God's ways. But even there, we don't create the change. That is God's work. We merely open our lives to him and allow him to make the changes.

When it comes to initiating a change of heart for other people, we have even less influence. It is not possible for us to cause another person to change. God did not create us for the purpose of, or with the ability to, change other people.

When he created us, he did not give us the capability to engage another person's spirit in a way that generates change. Every individual is created in the image of God as a self-conscious, free moral agent. Every person decides for himself or herself which course of life to take, and there is nothing you can do to make someone go another way. When a person does decide to open up to God, we can rejoice that God has performed a miracle using our lives as instruments. If they reject God, we will certainly be sad on that count. But in either case, we are not responsible for the outcome. We cannot take credit if they choose well, and we cannot take the blame if they choose poorly.

What we can do, though, is to become an instrument of God to confront the worldviews of those who are outside of the Kingdom. We are able to share a message with other people that will stimulate their imagination. This, then, becomes a catalyst for their change. When they are confronted with the worldview of the Kingdom, it is their turn to make a choice. When they choose to open their lives to God, he creates the change. Only God can activate the conversion in other people. But we can be his instruments to get them thinking about the truth that changes lives. And that is exactly God's plan for us. There are two elements of our involvement with God in this arena.

First, it is our solemn duty to understand the operation of the Kingdom. We cannot share what we ourselves do not understand. So our first order of business is to grasp the nature of the Kingdom and learn how to articulate the truth about it in ways that make sense to those outside of the Kingdom. Once we understand who God is, what reality is like, and how he wants us to operate in the material world, we must then take on the personal task of becoming a missionary to the non-Kingdom world. As we live out the truth of the Kingdom in our personal lives and articulate its truths, God takes that message and causes people to confront it in their hearts. At that point, they decide whether they will accept it or not.

The second element of our involvement goes back to our participation in material culture. Specific ways of communicating will catch the attention of specific individuals. Whether it relates to language, customs or belief systems, it is necessary to communicate worldview information in ways that reach people where they are. No individual on earth can reach into the lives of everyone. God uses people from every corner of human culture to touch the lives of those in various situations. We need to be sensitive to how God wants to use us and offer ourselves to him so that we can be his instruments to touch people so he can change them.

Our Responsibility

It is very clear in scripture that God wants every person to enter into a personal relationship with himself. As a result, he has initiated a general call to all mankind to come to him.

It is also very clear that everyone who accepts that first calling is given a second. That second one is to be God's instrument to share the worldview of the Kingdom and to be an active instrument in material culture to promote his purposes.

Digging Deeper

1. How deep is your personal conversion?
2. What about your life is radically different from what it was before you believed in God?

3. What tangible ways are you acting as an instrument of God to accomplish his purposes in the world?
4. What more should you be doing to be completely in line with his purpose for your life?

In my Christian experience I have served in all kinds of leadership positions, from my teenage years on. I have been to theological school and gotten my masters and doctorate degrees. I have been a church pastor, a missionary in two different countries and a church starter back in America. In other words, I have a pretty decent pedigree when it comes to my understanding of and involvement in Christian activity.

But there are various levels of understanding about everything in life, including our Christian development. For years I have been a committed, active and dedicated Christian worker. My commitment has not been shallow, either. I have been a true believer.

But I am still growing, and expect to continue that for the rest of my life. From time to time, even at my age, I really hit a growth spurt and come to a profound new level of understanding. Understanding Christian worldview and knowing how it relates to other worldviews has caused one of those spurts in me. As a result, I am now more confident and excited about living out my faith than I have ever been. I am convinced that every Christian can have this deepened level of faith if they will.

Chapter 12

Preparing Ourselves to Live in the Kingdom Culture

Therefore, I urge you, brothers, in view of God's mercy, to offer your bodies as living sacrifices, holy and pleasing to God—this is your spiritual act of worship. Do not conform any longer to the pattern of this world, but be transformed by the renewing of your mind. Then you will be able to test and approve what God's will is—his good, pleasing and perfect will.
Romans 12:1-2

What Are Kingdom Citizens Like?

When my wife and I lived in Japan, we decided to adopt a Japanese child and went through the legal processes to make that happen. For an adoption to take place, the Japanese government has a specified procedure that must be followed. First, there was a considerable amount of paperwork that we had to wade through. Then the government social services department had to conduct interviews of the birth mother and of us. When we finally finished going through that whole process, Ken officially, and legally, became a member of our family.

But hold on a minute. That was not the only process we had to go through. Since he was born as a Japanese citizen, we also had to go through a process to naturalize him as an American. That involved another ton of paperwork and red tape. But that still was not all. The procedure has since changed, but at that time we were required to actually bring him to American soil to finish the process. Just because we were American citizens and had legally adopted a baby, it did not mean that Ken was automatically an American citizen. We had to work through all the processes established by the various governmental bureaucracies to make it happen.

But what about after a person becomes a citizen? Is everything perfect, then? Of course not! We all know that there are various kinds of American citizens. Some are good citizens, and they fulfill the duties of citizenship with great enthusiasm. They vote, they are patriotic, they participate in civic activities, they are productive, they pay their taxes and so on. Others are more lax in their citizenship duties. They do what is required of them but nothing more than the minimum requirements. And, unfortunately, there are people who become bad citizens. These are people who deliberately break the law, evade taxes, don't vote and, in general, live a life that is harmful to the country.

When a person, like my son, is naturalized and becomes an American citizen, that person is not automatically a good and productive citizen. It is up to the individual to live a life that makes him one.

The issues involved in Kingdom citizenship are much the same. Anyone can become a Kingdom citizen by going through the process of establishing a personal relationship with God through Jesus Christ. But not everyone who takes this step becomes a good citizen once they are naturalized into the Kingdom.

It is like any membership group you can name. There will be those who take their membership seriously and take initiative to advance the interests of the group. They chair committees, they recruit new members, they work the fund raisers and do everything they can to make the group stronger.

Then, there are those who will be somewhat engaged. They attend all the meetings and occasionally serve on a committee, but they do nothing outside of the regular meeting times to promote the group.

Another faction, within most organizations, are those who are sporadic. They want their name associated with the group, but are only active as it is convenient for them. They only come to periodic functions, and never serve on any committees or work on group projects.

The last type of members are those who, once they join, never do anything. They don't even attend the membership meetings, much less participate in any projects. They joined at one time and are glad to accept the prestige of having their name on the membership roster, but never do anything to advance the interests of the group.

In the Kingdom of God, you will find the situation much like the membership group mentioned above. But there is one important difference—the Kingdom exists only on a spiritual level as individuals engage God in a personal relationship. This is not to imply that the matters of the Kingdom do not affect what goes on in the material world. There are many ways that it impacts our everyday lives. Perhaps the place we think of it most would be in our religious institutions— our churches, parachurch ministries, Bible study groups and so on. We think of these first because these are the places where most "Christian" activity tends to occur (the only places for some people).

But Kingdom activity actually occurs everywhere relationships exist. When we "give a cup of cold water in Jesus' name," when we share the gospel, when we give comfort or a helping hand with the intent of allowing God to reveal himself through us, or when we just put forth our best effort because we know God wants us to operate that way, the Kingdom of God is being inserted into the fabric of material society.

In the case of the Kingdom, the membership meeting is not church attendance, choir practice or discipleship training classes. It has to be thought of in more personal terms. Membership meetings only happen as people actually stand in the presence of God. This happens in private, and it happens when groups of people come together and meet God collectively. In other words, a church worship gathering should be a "membership meeting," but it may or may not be depending on the condition of the hearts of the individuals who are there.

Committee work would correspond to the strategic planning a person or group does with God in order to fulfill his/their mission in life. Kingdom projects reflect the various ministries that individuals and groups of believers might do to promote the goals of the Kingdom, based on their calling and the spiritual gifts given them by God. This ministry may be expressed through "Christian" institutions or through secular ones. Finally, recruitment corresponds to the efforts of Kingdom citizens to share citizenship opportunities with those who are outside of the Kingdom.

The level of activity that an individual chooses, whether in an earthly organization or in the Kingdom of God, is not something that just happens by chance—it is a choice. And the choice that a person makes produces a particular level of activity. Observe the activity and you will see the choice.

There are those who seem to naturally and easily slip into active involvement in the work of the Kingdom. There are others who are simply not interested in being involved at all. Both of those groups are small minorities, however. The large majority of people are not so actively engaged, though most at least have a sense that they ought to do more than they actually do. Whatever your own current level, you are not locked into it forever. If you have a desire to be a better Kingdom citizen, you can do it.

It All Starts With Purpose

You have to start with purpose. Everything you do, and the level of effort you put into it, emerges out of your life purpose. At this point, many people get confused. The idea that many have is that their purpose relates to some activity that God has called them to do. We certainly do find meaning when we are able to tap into the calling of God and involve ourselves in meaningful activity. But that relates more to the mission God wants to send us on. Purpose is something even more fundamental.

So what is the purpose of your existence in the Kingdom? Kingdom life centers around God, not around us. God created us to fulfill a particular purpose, and that purpose is to know him, to worship him, and to involve ourselves in activities that accomplish his purposes in the world. These things must come first! Only after we understand God's purpose and our place in it, can we begin to figure out our own mission. Only then are we able to begin the process of learning how it is to be played out in our own personal lives. Most people want to start with self, but this leads to self-centeredness. Kingdom living requires God-centeredness.

The Essential Relationship With God

The first step in fulfilling your purpose is to establish a personal connection with God. That is why he created us in the first place. God designed the entire material order, and humanity in particular, in a way that makes the relationship possible. He then established the mechanisms that allow it to happen.

Humanity was created in the image of God so that each person is spiritually capable of directly connecting with him. We were given the gift of self-awareness and the ability to choose our own destiny so that we could freely direct our love and allegiance as we wish. It is possible to choose otherwise, but the purpose, and desire, of God is that we choose him. Choosing him makes us a citizen of the Kingdom. Choosing not to enter a relationship with him excludes us from the Kingdom.

The relationship is established by our own personal invitation to God to make him a part of our life. But in order to do that we have to put ourselves in a position to be in his presence. Since part of the nature of God is absolute purity, we have to attain his level of purity in order to connect with him. It is not something that we can do on our own. We are flawed beings, and our very nature is permeated with imperfection and impurity.[1] This flawed nature has caused us to think thoughts, have attitudes and perform actions that put us outside of the realm of his presence.[2]

But he hasn't left us without hope. In his plan, God took the form of a human being—the man Jesus Christ. During his sojourn on earth, he satisfied the requirements of God's justice on our behalf by dying on the cross in our stead.[3] When we come to the place in our lives where we are willing to acknowledge and accept this gift, we can then choose to open our lives to him and invite him to connect his spirit to ours.[4]

But a relationship doesn't end when it begins. From the point of initial connection, it is God's purpose that we allow that relationship to grow.[5] It only grows as we actively work at understanding and living in the purpose we were created for, and in fulfilling the destiny that he has laid out for us individually. This requires that we continually keep our lives on a path that allows us to live in his presence. It requires that we actively seek to understand and fulfill the destiny that he has established for us.

Understanding Our Role in the Kingdom

So just what is that destiny? What is the role we have been called to fulfill in the Kingdom? In order to really understand this we have to learn to see things from a different perspective. Instead of seeing things the way we normally do, we need to take the perspective of a missionary.

Now this whole concept may seem strange if you have never stopped to think about it. After all, you have not been called to be a missionary, right? Well, if that is what you think, you are positively wrong! That is exactly what you have been called to. It's just that most people's concept of a missionary calling is incomplete.

Being a missionary does not necessarily mean you have to go overseas or to a different part of the country. Here we go again thinking in material terms. That may or may not be involved depending on the particular mission God has in mind for you. No, we have to understand that first and foremost we are citizens of the Kingdom of God. When we come to that understanding, we can see that our missionary service is to that part of the material world that is not connected with the Kingdom, no matter where they live.

Some people are especially called by God to go to different lands, and to cultures other than their own to do Christian work as a vocation. Others are called to do the work of the Kingdom under different circumstances—from the platform of a secular vocation, for instance. But regardless of the way one earns a living, everyone is called to be a missionary for the Kingdom! If this way of thinking has not yet caught your imagination, it is not your calling that is unclear, it is your understanding of that calling. God has clearly defined it, and it is up to you to find and understand it.

So how does that process play out in real life? There are a lot of ways we could characterize the activities that we have been called to, but there are three basic things that cover the possibilities.

The first role that we have as a citizen of the Kingdom is to be a *friend of God.* He created us for relationship with himself. So the thing we need to put our greatest emphasis on is to nurture that relationship. This means that we have to make the time to spend with him. Then we have to put forth the effort to eliminate the things from our lives that hinder our fellowship with him. Neither of these are small tasks. Both require a lot of personal discipline and the cultivation of a deep love for God.

The second role that we are called to take on as a Kingdom citizen is that of a *servant of God.* While we have the ability to choose our own way, we were not created to do that. God himself has created each individual to accomplish a specific work for the advancement of the Kingdom—a mission. When we first made the spiritual connection with God, he added something new to our lives—special spiritual abilities. These were not given to further our own desires, but to accomplish his specific purposes through us.

God's grand design is to get as many people as possible to enter a relationship with himself and become Kingdom citizens. His purpose continues in those individuals as he tries to help each one grow to perfection. He could have designed things in such a way that all of the work of building the Kingdom fell on his own shoulders. But he didn't. For some reason he decided to involve Kingdom citizens in the task. As we put ourselves under his authority and open ourselves to understand and accept his mission for our lives, we become able to fulfill the specific role of citizen that he has for us.

The third role that we are called on to fulfill is that of a *soldier of God.* The totality of existence consists of more than the material universe. There is a larger spiritual reality that exists beyond the touch of our senses. That larger spiritual reality is populated with spiritual beings who fall into one of two categories. The first class of beings are those who are aligned with God. They are committed to him and are active in carrying out his purposes. The second category are those who are arrayed against God. These beings are doing all that they can to thwart God's purposes.

A large part of their evil activity is to engage mankind and try to influence individual humans to rebel against God and reject him. A part of our work as Kingdom citizens is to do battle with these evil forces and to thwart that work in our personal lives, in the lives of other individuals and in the evil influences which emerge in society in general.

Making Preparation

So how do we know whether or not we are fulfilling our roles? Is there a measuring stick that can give us some indication of how we are doing? Indeed there is! Here we can use a very valuable principle. The principal states, "Examine your actions and you will see your beliefs." That is because actions always emerge out of beliefs. You virtually never do things that go against what you really believe. For some individuals, this can be a bit deceptive. Sometimes there is a difference between what we intellectually assent to and what we really believe. We all tend to have situations where we claim to believe something, but do not follow through with it in life. This is not true belief. True belief is experiential and is always followed by action. If you think that this statement is not true, you are deceiving yourself and your true beliefs are not what you think they are.

I don't pretend to be able to read the heart or intention of any other person. I can, though, be a fruit inspector. During the 2004 presidential campaign, John Kerry came out with the statement that, because of his religious beliefs, he was personally against abortion. He qualified that, however, by stating that his public policy decisions (and thus his votes in congress) were such that he felt that he needed to support a woman's "right to choose" to have an abortion, if she wanted one, over the protection of the life of an unborn child.

What he was demonstrating was two different sets of beliefs—one that indicates abortion is wrong and the other that abortion is okay. This situation got him into a lot of trouble during the campaign because the two beliefs are so contradictory. Only one could actually be expressed in his life, and he chose the abortion option. Regardless of his words, the action of his votes in congress demonstrated his true belief system.

It is certainly possible to be self-deceived, and many people are.

But make no mistake, your actions always reveal your most fundamental beliefs. There is a default position in our lives, and most people live by their default. But we can choose to follow the path God has prepared for us. That path requires that we make a deliberate effort to follow the ways of God. We have to prepare our minds and set our course, then live it out in life.

Digging Deeper

1. Do you consider yourself a citizen of God's Kingdom? What actions in your life could you cite to prove that point?

2. What is the most fundamental purpose of your life?

3. What do you do in daily life to fulfill that purpose?

4. What is lacking in your efforts to fulfill that purpose and what can you do to change it?

I am all about changing the world. I believe that it is a place created by God to achieve a particular purpose. But I also know that there are a lot of places where that purpose is not being expressed. I want to touch people's lives in such a way that they will experience the hand of God and be changed. I wish I were able to do so on my own, but I don't have the power to create that kind of change in other people. Only God can do that.

Still, I can be an agent of his Kingdom to try and get people's attention so that God can do his work in them. To do that, I have to live out the change he has made in me. Without that, no one will even pay any attention to what I am saying.

Understanding and living out the worldview of the Kingdom of God is the most exciting, meaningful and powerful experience I have ever had in my life. That being said, it is also one of the most difficult. There are obstacles everywhere. Most people don't like having their world-views disturbed, even if they are wrong. On top of that, Satan is actively working to influence us in the opposite direction—and his influence is quite difficult to combat.

Living in relationship with God, and living out his calling, is the most exciting life I can imagine. Nothing I have ever experienced outside of him even comes close.

Chapter 13

Steps to Developing
a Kingdom Mentality

*Therefore we do not lose heart. Though outwardly we are wasting away,
yet inwardly we are being renewed day by day. For our light and momen-
tary troubles are achieving for us an eternal glory that far outweighs them
all.* 2 Corinthians 4:16-17

A plumbing leak recently developed in my house. We discovered
it when my son walked into a room and heard water dripping onto a
cardboard box.

Since we were on the first floor of a two-story house and the drip
was coming from the ceiling, it was obvious that the problem originated on the second floor. Based on the location of the leak, we were
also able to determine fairly quickly that its source was the master
bathroom.

So after putting a bucket under the leak, we went upstairs to try
and identify the specific place the leak was coming from.
Unfortunately, there were no obvious telltale signs that would indicate
where the problem might be. There was no water on the floor, and we
could not hear the obvious sound of water flowing or spraying out of
any pipes. To figure it out, we had to go through a series of steps to
identify the problem.

My first step was to feel the floor around the base of the toilet. We
had experienced a different problem in the past which had a similar
result. In that case, water was leaking out of the tank of the toilet,
onto the floor and seeping under the toilet and down to the first floor.
This time, the tank was not leaking, but there was a trace of moisture
around the edge of the toilet.

Step two was to shut the water valve that fed the toilet to see if the source of the problem was in front or back of the valve. At first I was a bit concerned that it might be a leaky pipe inside the wall since the drip didn't stop right away. But, after a while it finally did stop, which let me know that the problem had something to do with the toilet itself.

The next step was to take the toilet up and check to see if the wax ring that the toilet sits on was leaking. As it turned out, that is exactly what the problem was. By going through the various steps, I was able to diagnose the problem and get it fixed.

As we think about the practical issues involved in conforming ourselves to the ways of God, there are also specific steps we can identify that will help us move in the direction we want to go. By following those steps we can develop the mentality that will help us move our lives toward becoming more effective Kingdom citizens.

Key Indicators of Good Kingdom Citizenship

It is not difficult to understand how to align our lives with the purposes of the Kingdom. It may be a struggle to implement our understanding, but the understanding itself is not so hard.

First of all, when we put the Kingdom as the highest priority in our lives, we will make sure that our relationship with God is in good shape. So look at your life. Do you spend time with God? Do you put your relationship with him above your work, your studies, your social life, your sports, your hobbies, your_____ (you name it)? This is not meant to imply that these various areas of life are contrary to God's purposes in and of themselves. But our priorities have to be right. If your walk with God is not an integral part of every aspect of your life, and if you don't consult and obey him on all the activities in your life, you have a problem in this area. When you put the Kingdom of God first, your relationship with him will be in good shape!

Another key indicator is that, when you put the Kingdom of God first, you will nurture the "spirits" that God has entrusted to you. That's right, God has entrusted the spiritual lives of certain people to you. This does not mean that you can live another person's life for them. It also doesn't mean that you are responsible if they choose to walk a path that takes them away from God. But there are certain people you have influence with and you are charged, by God, to be an example and a positive influence on them.

This principle is to be expressed in the family. If you are a husband, you are responsible for leading your family to know and worship God, and to guide them into fellowship with the body of Christ. If you are a wife, you are responsible for being the supporting spiritual pillar and for creating an atmosphere which facilitates the spiritual growth of the family. If you are a parent, you are responsible for providing the influence for your children that will lead them to a relationship with God.

The principle is also evident in other relationships. You are responsible for living a life that reflects well on Kingdom citizenship. You are responsible for living your life in such a way as to be a positive influence and role model for those people you know who do not yet have a personal relationship with God.

To be sure, you are not responsible for the decisions other people make in their lives. But, you can know that the Kingdom of God has first place in your life when you are consistently nurturing the relationships God has entrusted to you.

The third key indicator that lets you know when you have put the Kingdom above your material culture is that the activities you participate in actually serve to further your God-given mission as their first objective. How does this play out in life? When you go to work, to school, to play, engage in sports, etc., your relationships and your actions demonstrate that your life is being used to point people toward a relationship with God.

There are plenty of actions in this category that can become indicators of your commitment to God. Some, for instance, relate to how you use your material resources. When you spend your money, do you spend all of it in a way that fulfills your mission? That doesn't mean that you "give it all to the poor" or to the church. But there is a way God wants you to use it and a way he doesn't want you to use it. Do you ever even think about that? Does the way you drive your car or use your house serve to fulfill your mission? Do the websites you visit further the work of the Kingdom in your life? Do the establishments you frequent and the language you use reflect the fulfillment of God's mission in your life?

God has selected and spiritually equipped you to influence your world. You know that you are fulfilling your role when your actions serve to fulfill the mission.

Training Ourselves To Be Good Citizens

The fact that we were created to be citizens of the Kingdom, and that we have the ability to be good citizens, does not mean that it automatically happens. We have to make choices in life, and the choices we have made up until now have gotten us to the place we currently are. If we are good citizens, it is because we have made choices that have brought us to that place. If we are not good Kingdom citizens, it is because we have made choices that have taken us in a different direction.

Spiritual Training Decisions

From our current station in life, we have to make good choices in two areas. First we have to choose to produce good spiritual fruit. Spiritual fruit are the spiritual characteristics that can be seen in our lives. The Bible tells us that the fruit of a life lived for God are such things as love, joy, peace, patience, kindness, goodness, faithfulness, gentleness and self-control. We do not automatically display these characteristics. We have to choose them and allow God to work in and through us, then put out effort to make it happen.

The second area where we have to make good choices is in developing our spiritual abilities and using them to accomplish the mission God has prepared for us individually. God has created each person to accomplish particular tasks in life and has equipped us to do them. These tasks certainly involve material accomplishments, but these are only secondary. The primary focus of this mission is spiritual. It involves developing ourselves to be better kingdom citizens and touching the lives of others to help them do the same. All spiritual gifts are given for this reason alone. If we are going to become good Kingdom citizens, we have to choose to use our spiritual abilities for the purpose they were given, and we have to put forth effort to make it happen.

Spiritual Training Facilities

There are places we can train to become better at producing good fruit and in using our spiritual gifts. These places are really not so much physical places as they are "opportunity places."

One place is in the church family. It must be stressed, here, that the church is essentially a network of relationships before it is an institution. Since we are physical beings living in a physical world, we must have some physical or institutional expression of the network. But the relationships must be primary. By spending time together with our spiritual family network, we are able to mentor and be mentored, teach and be taught, encourage and be encouraged, strengthen and be strengthened. We do this through personal relationships, Bible study, spiritual training opportunities and by reaching out to others in ministry activities.

Another "opportunity place" for spiritual training is in our own personal study. There are lots of books, tapes, and courses we can work through that teach us how to become better Kingdom citizens. We must also take personal time and effort to pray, study the Bible and meditate—that is, to spend time with God.

Finally we must take our spiritual growth out into the physical life we live. We can apprentice with someone to supplement what we have learned in a classroom environment. But we can also get out there on our own and use the fruit and the gifts God has given us to touch the world. We learn and grow in the process of doing.

Spiritual Training Regimen

There is one more thing that we have to come to grips with. It is not enough to learn about all of the growth possibilities. It is not enough to learn all of the growth and ministry skills. It is not even enough to put ourselves into a position to use them all. We have to get on a personal spiritual growth regimen that is ongoing, or we will begin to fall back.

To move past the level of "beginner," we have to develop our spiritual fruit and gifts to a very high level. It can be compared to physical conditioning. When an individual wants to perform well in some sport, it is necessary to get conditioned for that activity. This is true whether it is just walking around the block or playing linebacker on a professional football team. There is a basic conditioning that has to take place. The muscles have to be strengthened and the lung-power developed.

But how many people have determined to get in shape, done it, then, after a short time, have quit and gotten out of shape again? It happens all the time. I have done it myself, and I imagine you have, too. The person who just wants to "be athletic" can do that. But the person who "is an athlete" will train in a way that keeps them perpetually fit and ready to perform at any time.

It is possible to learn all the right stuff and perform some good Kingdom activity once in a while. But the person who wants to be a good Kingdom citizen trains continually to the very end of life.

Accomplishing Good Kingdom Citizenship

Being a good citizen of the Kingdom of God is not merely a matter of what you do. Rather, it is expressed in who you are. If you are a good citizen, that will automatically be expressed in what you do. The "being" almost always comes before the "doing." As a follower of Jesus Christ in the Kingdom of God, there should come a time when you make a mental and spiritual shift. *You need to shift away from thinking of yourself as a person who is a believer and who has a job to perform, to one who is a Kingdom citizen with a lifelong calling to fulfill.* You might want to take a little time to contemplate that last sentence. It has profound implications well beyond what you might imagine.

Every believer is called by God to share the gospel of Jesus Christ. That doesn't mean that everyone is called to become a professional church leader. Only a few are called to that task. The rest have other places and groups where they are supposed to plug in and exercise their influence for the Kingdom. Good Kingdom citizens are going to find their calling, develop their gifts, grow their fruit, then get out there and influence the world.

Digging Deeper

1. What in your life indicates how good a Kingdom citizen you are?
2. What specific ways are you training yourself to become a more effective Kingdom citizen?

For some reason, I have never wanted to be a vigorous social activist. I have, from time to time, been known to write a letter to the editor or to my congressman, and have even refused to buy from certain companies that were working against what I believe in. So it is not that I have no social involvement at all. But I have not been one to join activist groups, march in demonstrations, or the like.

This does not mean that I don't believe in activism. Sometimes it is important to actively and visibly stand up and be counted; I wouldn't eliminate that option for myself under the right conditions.

But underneath the activism, we must always maintain our "soul." We shouldn't become an activist just to make culture conform to the ways of God. Whatever cause we pursue must be to further the purposes of God. We are looking to transform culture from the inside out, not simply to change its outward appearance.

My personal calling focuses more on preparing other people to live fully in Kingdom culture. Some others have a calling that involves them more directly in the activism itself. Regardless of any specific calling, we must all prepare ourselves to be used as instruments of God to fulfill his purposes through us.

Chapter 14

The Culture War
Is a Different Kind of War

Finally, be strong in the Lord and in his mighty power. Put on the full
armor of God so that you can take your stand against the devil's schemes.
For our struggle is not against flesh and blood, but against the rulers,
against the authorities, against the powers of this dark world and against
the spiritual forces of evil in the heavenly realms. Therefore put on the full
armor of God, so that when the day of evil comes, you may be able to
stand your ground, and after you have done everything, to stand.
Ephesians 6:10-13

There are "armchair quarterbacks" all over the world. These are
people who take an interest in a topic, learn all about it, sit back and
watch other people participate in the activity. Then, when it is all finished, they critique the performance.

The expression has its origin with people who sit in their living
rooms on Saturday and Sunday and watch football games. After the
game, they go around telling everyone what the coach and the quar-
terback should have done.

Nowadays this phrase is used in other areas of life to express a similar concept. It could be media analysts who give their opinion on how
a business should have operated to avoid financial or legal problems,
political analysts who criticize politicians they disagree with, or even
art critics who give their opinion on why a painting, movie or play was
no good.

There is no doubt that some of the people who do this have some
good points to make. But there is a fatal flaw in this kind of activity.
Armchair quarterbacks have not been in the game. They can sit back
in their overstuffed armchairs, in the air-conditioned comfort of their

107

living rooms, guzzling their drinks and dipping their chips without any of the pressure of having to perform in the game. There are no consequences to their analysis, so they can make any criticism they want with virtual impunity. They also have the advantage of not having to make any evaluations until after they see the result. Ninety-nine percent of armchair quarterbacks would crumble and fold if they had to be the one responsible for actually making things happen in real life. That is because they don't have the specific knowledge, training or experience to actually get the job done.

There is probably no place in life where this concept is demonstrated more than when dealing with spiritual matters. If you were to approach almost any stranger and ask that person how to most effectively live a good spiritual life, virtually everyone would give you their philosophy of life and tell you why the world is in such a mess. But if you were to dig a little deeper and question how they, themselves, are working to make things better, you would find indignation on top of ignorance. This is not an exaggeration. Most people are not really interested in playing the spiritual "game"! They simply want to sit back and criticize those who do.

But our life is not a game in which we are able to simply sit back, observe, and critique. Everyone is involved in spiritual activity whether they want to be or not—whether they even realize it or not. It is an integral part of living life, and there is only one way to get out of the choices that are required. That is to step out of time and into eternity. Until then, we are all actively involved in life.

We fight a spiritual war when we go to work, when we come home from work, when we go out to play or to study, when we talk to people, and even when we sit at home and watch TV. Everything we think and do contributes to who we are becoming and influences how we affect the lives of those we interact with. As we go about our everyday lives, we are either building ourselves up or tearing ourselves down. We are either leading people toward the Kingdom or away from it. There is no middle ground.

We have covered a lot of territory so far in attempting to understand the nature of the Kingdom of God. We have talked about what it is, who is involved, how individuals are involved and many other things. But there is one thing left, and that is to see how we can actually live out life in the Kingdom. How do we go about actually fighting the culture wars?

The Real War Is Not the Culture War

So how do we do that? It is certainly a valid principle that no matter where specific evil influences come from, it is proper to work against them. But the most important part of the fight is not against the material cultural expressions that evil produces. Ultimately, the war is not a material war. Many of the battles may be fought in our physical world, but the war itself is spiritual. You can stamp out a particular behavior in one area, but it will appear again somewhere else, and some new one will soon emerge where the old one was.

The war, itself, is the effort to capture the hearts and minds of individuals. People live according to what they believe in their hearts. If we want to win this war, we can't simply fight culture. We have to go one step further and fight worldviews. We have to understand the assumptions that underlie evil expressions in a cultural context and expose the evil for what it is. We have to be about convincing people that a connection with God is a more desirable way to live life than not having a connection with him.

We have to engage people at the level of belief. We have to be able to refute the beliefs that they hold which lead to evil behavior. Then we have to express the principles of the Kingdom which lead to a life in relationship with God. If we intend to be intentional participants in this war, there are some very specific things that we need to educate ourselves on.

First, we have to learn the concepts and principles of the various worldviews. The underlying assumptions of Naturalism, Animism, Far Eastern thought and most forms of Theism are simply wrong. But if we don't know what the beliefs are, we are certainly not going to be able to explain them to anyone else. How can we rightfully enter into the mindset and life of the people of a different culture if we don't make the effort to learn the worldview that informs their choices? We can't!

We have to spend time studying people, engaging their culture, and especially getting one-on-one with them so we can know them as individuals. And the reason it is important is not so that we can become better educated and able to win arguments. It is because the eternal destiny of these individuals depends on them knowing and following the truth.

Secondly, we need to know the assumptions of Relational Revelation. This is God's revealed truth concerning how a person is able spend eternity in relationship with him. We certainly cannot make a person believe the truth, but we should, at least, be able to explain it if the opportunity ever came up. These assumptions include the truth that reality is made up of a material and a spiritual world which God designed in a particular way for a particular reason. It includes an explanation of the message of how God took the form of the man Jesus Christ, lived a perfect life, and died as a sacrifice to pay the penalty for the unholiness of mankind. And finally it includes the truth that a person not only has to believe this truth intellectually, but must also go the next step to turn away from evil ways and personally accept this sacrifice as a gift from God in order to enter into a relationship with him.

Finally, we have to move beyond mere knowledge and actually live our lives based on these truths. We have to live a life that is consistent with the revelation and become active instruments of God who share it with those who are not yet part of the Kingdom. And we must do it all according to the principles and values of the Kingdom. We have to be bold but not obnoxious. We must realize that the ends do not justify the means. We have to live out the principles and values of the Kingdom as we struggle against the forces of the evil one.

But what is the typical person's pattern of life? Our usual pattern is to develop our schedule around all of the things we want or think we need to do, then get together with God if we have some extra time. Usually we operate within our family based on everyone's varied activities; then, once in a while, we throw in a spiritual development activity. Most of the time we fill up our lives with business and social activities and only occasionally give a few minutes to God—if it works into our schedule.

All of this is completely backwards. God has to be first. The Kingdom has to be first. And that does not mean we merely try and fit our personal, family and other activities around religious ones. Rather, it means we are to build our whole life on the foundation of the Kingdom, not on the foundation of our material culture.

All of this can be done. Sometimes the work is slow. Sometimes it is frustrating. Sometimes it seems to be absolutely hopeless. But our only task is to be faithful to the King.

So Why is the Culture War Important?

If the real war is in the spiritual realm, then what is the urgency in trying to make things go a certain way in the physical world? Why don't we just put all of our effort into trying to convince people concerning spiritual things? After all, if they change their worldview, there is certain to be a change in the way they relate to the world, right?

This is absolutely true. The only problem is, a large percentage of people in the world do not accept the worldview of Relational Revelation, and the direction in which those people are taking the world has some very serious consequences. We who are Christians have no choice but to operate in the material arena and cannot avoid having to deal with those consequences, whatever they may be. But even as we engage in the culture war, we are not simply deciding, on our own, what is important or what kind of response we ought to have. The Revelation spells out a right way to think and live and gives us important reasons why we need to be engaged on the cultural level.

The Culture War and the Purposes of God

God created material reality for a purpose. One important aspect of that purpose was to provide an arena in which mankind could grow, develop and connect with God.

However, it is possible for humanity to mess up what God is trying to do. By establishing governments that oppress people and by creating an environment that is accepting of things that are evil, nasty, dirty, and just plain wrong, the world becomes a place where it is more difficult for people to follow the purposes of God. Certainly we are able to operate in the middle of any kind of evil that may exist, and can even be a good influence in it. But a bad environment makes it much more likely that people will fall away from God rather than move toward him.

For instance, the easy access to pornography on the internet has led to higher and higher levels of crime, psychological problems and broken homes. When I was a child, pornography was available, but was not so easy to come by. There were magazines like Playboy around, but it took a special effort for someone to go to the store, buy it and keep it hidden. Now pornography is all pervasive on the internet. As a result, the number of people who view it and the negative impact it is having on society, such as child molestation, broken marriages, sexual addictions, etc., is exploding—all because it is so accessible. Pornography was around long before the internet even existed. But its easy access and wide acceptance has created an environment where more and more people have been involved with it, and the number of resulting problems have been going through the roof.

Another example is the common acceptance of sexual relations outside of marriage. In previous generations, marriage was commonly accepted as the only legitimate place to participate in sexual relations. This is not to say that premarital sex, the infidelity of a marriage partner, homosexuality and other deviant sexual relationships were not around before. They certainly were. But they were considered by society in general, even by the people who participated, as wrong. This general attitude tended to have a depressing effect on the number of people who were "immoral" in those ways. But in our day, sex outside of marriage is largely viewed as a recreational activity. It is portrayed on TV and in movies as the normal state of affairs. And, as more and more people have bought into this way of thinking, the incidence of divorce, unfaithfulness in marriage, homosexual behavior, sexually transmitted diseases, and so on, has gone up.

These are just two examples. We could go on and on talking about the disastrous effects on society of alcohol, tobacco and drug abuse, overeating, the decline in the way society values life, gambling, unethical business practices, profanity and many other things. The more that bad behaviors are accepted within a culture, the more they are practiced. The more they are practiced, the more we see individuals, families and communities falling apart.

If for no other reason than to maintain an orderly society, it is important for individuals to understand the forces in culture that are destructive and to actively work against them. There always have been, and always will be, people who are more interested in satisfying their own personal desires than in making sure society operates in a manner that provides the best chance for the next generation to make it. Those who are interested in a stable, ongoing society have to make sure their values are injected into the mix. If we don't, our children will grow up in an environment where bad behavior and evil thinking are normalized and where more and more of them follow that road.

The Command of God

But our inclination to work for the betterment of culture is more than just a practical issue. God, in his revelation, has given us the responsibility to do it. In Genesis 1:28-30, God specifically gave mankind the responsibility to subdue the earth and to have dominion over it. In other words, the owner of the world (God) made mankind the manager of world operations. We have an actual duty to work and make sure that things are operating in a manner that goes along with his purposes. When some people make efforts to move things in the wrong direction, we are responsible to try and make corrections.

While the real war is the struggle for hearts and minds, we still cannot give up the world. It is one of the battlegrounds on which the war is fought. God created the world for a purpose and wants us to actively work to make sure that an environment is in place which allows that work to get done. We have to fight to accomplish God's purposes in our temporary earthly existence, but always with a view to the eternal.

Understanding the Enemy

In any war there is an opponent. We need to get this one right in order to be effective in fighting our skirmishes. Since we are so actively engaged in the physical world, it is easy to get so involved in the struggle to maintain a godly culture that we lose sight of what is really at stake. We have to know something about who we are up against if we want to be effective in our fight.

We have already established that the Kingdom is spiritual, not physical. We are not out to change the way people eat and dress. We are looking to lead people to a connection with God so they can have a way of believing, thinking and behaving which is consistent with their purpose for being. So the real enemy is not the culture. When we dig in to fight the culture war, we have to be sure we are looking behind the outward forms of culture to get at the real culprit.

In an operating environment that is spiritual, the enemy is also spiritual. God is a personal being who is the epitome of good, love, right and justice. The enemy is the exact opposite. Satan is a personal being who is the very essence of evil, hate, unrighteousness and injustice. He is a being who operates in the spiritual world and is attempting to undo everything that God is working to accomplish. He is personally engaging people, spirit to spirit, in order to influence them in ways that cause them to destroy their own lives and take other people with them. He is not some abstract concept of evil. He is a personal being who operates in the realm of spirit and is able to engage the spirits of human beings on a personal level as he tries to influence their thoughts and behavior.

The term *influence* is used here intentionally. Influence is a force that is applied from the outside for the purpose of persuading a person to change thoughts and behavior. Still, there is nothing that makes a person follow any particular influence. In the context of our spiritual war, Satan's influence is an outside force and an objective reality. But the decision to follow it or not is made by each individual. Even though some forms of influence are quite powerful, and we might not like the consequences of giving in to it (or not giving in), no one can say they were forced to follow any particular influence. Ultimately, we decide individually.

When we see individuals engaging in self-destructive behavior, it is because they have given in to the enemy who is applying evil influence in order to try and lead them in that direction. When we see people acting selfishly and hatefully toward other people, we are witnessing another form of submission to that influence. When we see people killing, torturing, maiming and enslaving other people, it is again an outward expression of that evil influence not being resisted in physical life.

This evil influence is not typically applied like we see it in the movies where a demon enters an individual, takes over their life, and causes them to go around with spit drooling down their chin and a wild glow in their eyes as they pillage and destroy everything and everyone they see. Rather, it is done in the same way as the influence that comes from God—by spiritual communication. (For a more complete treatment of this communication process, read Praying is not for Wimps). We are spiritual beings and we interact in the spiritual realm by making our own decisions (either intentionally or by default) regarding which spiritual beings we will pay attention to. If it is not God, then it is Satan. There are no other choices.

When most people think about the work of evil in the world, they think of people like Hitler, Stalin, Saddam Hussain and other monsters who have been instruments of the slaughter of millions of people. And certainly the lives of these individuals are dramatic evidence of the work of evil forces in the world. But the large percentage of evidence that Satan is at work in the world is not the really dramatic stuff. Rather, it is in the daily decisions that individuals make about life direction.

Sure we see examples where killing and torture have become an actual part of a culture. And where these elements have gained that kind of grip it is important to actually try and change the material culture. But most of the evil elements that exist in culture are in the thoughts and behavior of ordinary individuals.

Why would a person view taking drugs as an acceptable activity? It is not because it is part of being an American (or a Dutchman or a NASCAR fan or a Democrat). If a person accepts this activity it is because a personal moral decision has been made to accept the influences of evil that have been vying for his or her attention. We could make the same observation about every other expression of evil that we see in the world—things like lying, cheating, using foul language, spouse and child abuse, homosexuality, abortion, murder, hate and on and on. None of these are essential parts of any material culture. The degree to which they are accepted is simply an indication of the degree to which evil spiritual influences have become a part of the lives of the people in that culture. But getting rid of the evil does not destroy any culture.

What Determines Victory?

In preparing to do battle in the culture war, we also must define victory. How do we know when we are doing the right thing? How can we judge whether or not we are making progress? Are we victorious when abortion is no longer legal? Have we won when marriage is legally defined as one man and one woman?

As important as these outcomes might be, there is no single issue that society can get right which will ever win the war. If we really want to understand the reality of the situation, all we have to do is look back once again at what happened in the Prohibition struggle. Evil is not a physical entity and cannot be defeated by physical means. We struggle in the physical arena because that is where we live. But victory only happens when enough people in a particular culture have entered into a relationship with God, so that society willingly moves in the direction of God's purposes.

There have been times in history when that has happened. History records great spiritual movements when massive numbers of people turned to God and crime and immorality nearly disappeared—for a time. But what happened after that? Evil reared its ugly head again and the next generation had to fight the battles again.

We humans are incapable of actually achieving victory. But God is able and wants to use us as instruments in the fight. As we are faithful in living life in a way that promotes God's purposes, he engages people on a personal level and does his work in their lives. Victory, then, happens when a culture turns to God.

Digging Deeper

1. What are the specific issues that you face in culture which are working against the purposes of God?
2. Do you feel that it is important for you, personally, to get involved in fighting the things that work against the purposes of God?
3. What do you do to engage the culture war in your physical culture?
4. What hinders you from being more involved in engaging your culture in order to advance the Kingdom of God?

I may not be the type of activist that protests in front of abortion clinics or works on petition drives, but I am an activist just the same. I believe that God is a real individual and that I am able to have a personal relationship with him. I believe that he has a purpose for my life, and has given me a calling I can discern and follow. I am committed to engaging in that calling in order to promote the expansion of his Kingdom.

I am convinced that you, too, have that kind of calling from God. Your specific mission is different than mine, but it is just as real. And it has the same purpose as its end—the expansion of the Kingdom of God.

Everyone who is really serious about living out their faith in Christ needs to take a deeper look at the way their activism for the Kingdom is displayed. For some it will be very "activistic." For others it will be a more subtle, behind the scenes, type of activism. But every believer needs to be an activist for God.

Gaining a deeper understanding of your own worldview and a commitment to adopting more and more of the worldview of the Kingdom are important first steps. They will fortify your faith in a way that causes you to be more determined to partner with God to accomplish his purposes.

Chapter 15

How to Fight the Culture War

For though we live in the world, we do not wage war as the world does. The weapons we fight with are not the weapons of the world. On the contrary, they have divine power to demolish strongholds. We demolish arguments and every pretension that sets itself up against the knowledge of God, and we take captive every thought to make it obedient to Christ. 2 Corinthians 10:3-5

It is time, now, to really get down to cases. What do we do with the evil expressions of culture that we find before us every day? What is the best way for us, as Kingdom citizens, to go about fighting the evil influences that make their way into our material culture? Should we form groups and organize protests and boycotts? Should we confront individuals about their evil behavior? Should we run for office and try to change the laws? Should we crash organizations that support evil behavior and shout them down? Should we take up arms and physically fight against them? Should we run people who have different viewpoints out of our community?

In 1998 anti-abortion activist James Kopp was charged with the murder of abortion doctor Barnett Slepian in New York. Kopp considered abortion to be the murder of innocent unborn children. It seems that Slepian had been performing abortions since the eighties and was often the target of anti-abortion protesters. Given the beliefs of Mr. Kopp, that abortion is murder, was he right in killing the abortion doctor to save the unborn?

The short answer to that question is no! There are appropriate ways and inappropriate ways to fight the culture war. God has structured Kingdom morality to align with his character. While the killing of the unborn may go against God's ways, murder of the already born

119

does, too. It is not appropriate to go against God's character in order to accomplish something in line with it. In other words, the ends do not justify the means.

So, how should we answer all of the questions which were broached at the beginning of the chapter? Depending on the particular situation, any of the scenarios above might be an appropriate response—or they might be inappropriate. In any case, we need to be active in figuring out the appropriate way to be the instruments of God in the fight against evil. We need to work against evil in whatever ways we can while still displaying the character of God in our own lives.

Evil expressions in culture are not only offenses to us as individuals and to God, but they actually do damage to the physical and spiritual lives of individuals who have to be exposed to them. I have heard it argued that smoking pot, for instance, is a victimless activity. Some might say the same thing about homosexuality, overeating, profanity, sexual relations outside of marriage, smoking tobacco, pornography and so on. But the evidence shows otherwise. Every one of the activities that people tout as "victimless" actually create victims. In fact, there are three sets of victims that we see whenever evil activities are practiced.

The first is *society at large*. When evil activities are normalized by a culture, it sucks more and more people into them and leads to greater destruction and degradation in the society.

The second victim is the *person practicing the activity*. Every single one of the things listed above, as well as any other behavior that goes against the ways of God, causes massive destruction in the lives of the people who practice them. That destruction takes the form of physical, mental, emotional and spiritual ruin as they live their daily lives. And in the eternal realm, since God requires purity as a condition for being in his presence, whenever a person makes a deliberate decision to walk in an ungodly direction, a resolve has been established that moves that one toward an eternity in that part of the spiritual realm where God is absent.

The third set of victims are *other people whose lives are negatively af-*

fected by the decline of the person who is practicing the activity. It may be a child who is emotionally and spiritually damaged when parents divorce. It may be family members who are hurting emotionally as they watch someone they love become self-destructive. It may be an employer who is getting lower productivity as an employee deteriorates. It may be children or young people who are led in the wrong direction as they look to that person as a role model.

Because the stakes are so high, it is imperative that we take note of the specific evil influences that have taken root in our physical culture and work at snatching them out. We need to help people avoid evil, and we need to help those who have already stumbled to get their lives back. To do this we have to be actively engaged in causes and ministries that work against evil influences. It is good to work with the homeless, to support the organizations who are helping young women avoid abortions, to help rehabilitate those who have been in prison, and to work against smoking, drug misuse and alcohol abuse.

The one thing we have to keep in mind, though, is that all of these things are only outward expressions of the real problem. They are not the problem itself. While working to rid society of its evils, we have to be careful that we do not view the elimination of a particular expression of evil as an end in itself. We have to look deeper to find the root cause and put our greatest energy there, while still striving to eliminate the outward expressions.

So, What Do We Do?

Up to this point we have come to some pretty important understandings. We have identified the various life patterns of the people who live in the world and have seen how these various worldviews affect the way we live. We have tagged the worldview that most closely reflects the way our world operates. We have learned that the various expressions of worldview show up in material cultures and that some are good and some are bad. We have seen that there are times when we need to take measures to root out the evil expressions of culture that rear their ugly heads. And finally, we have seen that, even though we need to be engaged in guarding our culture from evil, the ultimate solution is not in changing outward expressions of culture, but in changing the hearts of individuals.

All of this is important information, but means absolutely nothing if we don't take action to allow God to do the work of his Kingdom through our lives. So, how do we do it? Well, there are several concrete steps we can take. Let's look at those now.

Start With Self

All Kingdom activity is built on the foundation of a relationship with God. It is one thing to know what is right and to tell other people what that is. It is something else, altogether, to make it a reality in our own lives.

If we want to be instruments of God in the process of extending his Kingdom, we have to do several things. *First of all we have to live holy lives.* We have to decide that we are willing to pay the price to put aside all the evil and evil influences in our own lives. This includes all the wrongs that we are personally attached to, whether they be overt actions we take or actions that should be in our lives and have been neglected. The most important thing is to put ourselves in a position to live in relationship with God.

It also includes becoming spiritually strong enough to resist the temptations that are directed toward us from other people. There are all kinds of people around us who want to see us fail in our spiritual walk. It helps them feel justified in continuing their own life of wrong-doing. Whether it is co-workers who put you down, colleagues who try to get you involved in activities that are wrong, a spouse who tries to pull you away from fellowship with the church body or other family members and social acquaintances who push you to give up your faith, you have to develop yourself to be spiritually strong enough to withstand the onslaught.

The second thing we have to do is to take up our identity as agents in the building up of the Kingdom. It is one thing to enter a personal relationship with Christ and become a Kingdom citizen. It something else again to see Kingdom citizenship as our highest allegiance and as the force that animates and motivates our lives.

When God allowed us to become naturalized citizens of his domain, he assigned us a mission. The specific mission is different for each individual, but every one centers on the building up of the Kingdom. In order to accomplish our mission, we have to discern what it is and learn how to do the job. We have to educate ourselves about the Kingdom, about worldviews and about culture.

Once we have that knowledge base, it is then necessary to become active in carrying out our assigned task. The desire of God is for new citizens to join the kingdom and for existing citizens to be strengthened. Our responsibility is obedience to the calling.

So the first thing is to take care of yourself. When you do that you are ready to move on to the next part of your Kingdom responsibility.

Take Care of Your Family

The family is the first human institution God established when he created mankind. *We cannot fulfill our Kingdom duties unless we are doing our part to take care of family.* Every member of the family has a role to play, and the faithfulness of each person in fulfilling their role determines how effectively the family functions.

This is important because the family is the underlying strength of every culture. If the foundation of the family is strong, the culture has a basis for moving forward into the future. If the foundation is weak, the culture is on its way to crumbling. That is why issues such as divorce, sexual relations outside of marriage, how marriage is defined, care of widows and orphans, homosexuality, and the care and education of our children are so important.

The husband has the responsibility to be the leader of the family. This does not mean he should be a dictator! It is not a "do what I say do" proposition. Many people get this wrong with disastrous effects. A good leader sets the direction and keeps things on track while enabling all the followers to reach their highest potential. It is not the place where one goes to be waited on, but is the position of highest responsibility and sacrifice. The husband is responsible for setting an atmosphere in the family where the wife and children can thrive. When the husband creates this climate, the family is in great shape to become a strong block in the culture's foundation which will allow it to continue and flourish.

The wife has the responsibility for being the nurturer of the family. This does not mean that she is not allowed to work outside the home or participate in activities where she can fully express her abilities. We are talking about the role in the family, not the particular outside activities she participates in. There are certain things that are typically more suited to the nature of women and which are essential if the family is to thrive. Regardless of the other outside activities in which the wife involves herself, she does need to provide an atmosphere within the family that is supportive and nurturing for the husband and the children.

A husband and wife together are responsible for raising their children in a way that helps them to grow up to be responsible and productive citizens of the culture. Children do not develop the qualities they need in a vacuum. If the parents do not provide the right environment and disciplines for growth, the kids will grow up at a huge disadvantage. One of the essential character traits that an individual needs is the ability to be self-disciplined. Parents give this to their children by creating limits and boundaries, then gradually expanding those boundaries as they are able to handle more. *Parenting is not about producing offspring, it is about taking the offspring they have and guiding them to maturity.* Parents who neglect this responsibility are contributing to the breakdown of their culture.

Children, too, have a role. Even though they don't have the perspective, while they are young, to understand all of the reasons parents do what they do, they are responsible for trusting their parents to help them grow. This is not something that comes naturally. It is up to the parents not only to teach them what to do, but why to do it. *Children who are respected this way, and who are raised to be self-disciplined and responsible, will ensure the strength of the culture into the future.*

The reason this is mentioned in this discussion is because different worldviews result in different ways of thinking about family and of living out family life. A worldview that sees no ultimate meaning and purpose in human existence will accept any formulation of family as long as it seems functional. Of course using this way of thinking, the concept of "functional" also has no moral foundation—it simply becomes what the members of society want to make of it. A worldview that sees the family as a lineage of gods will fight for a kind of structure that maintains the status quo. And, as evidenced by current events in Western cultures, many committed Naturalists see no problem with such things as homosexual marriage or even incest with one's children.

But God's purpose for the family is for it to be an environment in which everyone is encouraged to connect with God, and where each person is allowed to reach their highest potential. It is only as the family develops in the right way that a culture is established on a foundation that will be strong for the future.

So, after taking care of ourselves individually, *the second requirement is to take care of our family.* Every person must actively work at developing the attitudes, skills and lifestyle that help them fulfill their appointed roles in the family.

There are a lot of issues going on in modern society which degrade the family. There is unfaithfulness to the marriage partner, divorce, domestic violence, child abuse and exploitation, pornography (especially kiddy porn), pedophilia, the killing of the unborn and the attempt to redefine marriage, just to name a few. We need to be aware of these issues and do all we can to strengthen the family and to work against the things that tear it down.

Every person needs to be actively engaged in making sure that all of the family members are vitally connected to God. Become the spouse you need to become. Become the parent you need to become. Become the child you need to become. It is your calling from God to fulfill your responsibilities in this area.

Take Care of Your Community

Let's once again make the main point the main point! If we ever want to be effective in accomplishing the work of the Kingdom of God, *our primary focus has to be on worldview issues, not on issues related to changing the culture.* Accomplish the Kingdom tasks, and the culture issues will automatically move in the right direction.

That being said, *we are still responsible for helping maintain order in the culture by working against the things that degrade it*. First, let's look at how we can promote the Kingdom worldview in our community, then we can address how to deal with the specific issues that are expressed in the culture.

How do we promote the Kingdom worldview? The answer to that lies in how we live our lives. We have already seen how it is necessary to start with our own beliefs and values. But intellectual affirmation is not enough. We have to stake ourselves to godly values as we live life. We need to be firm enough in our worldview belief that we are willing, and able, to take a public stand for our faith in Jesus Christ.

This does not mean we should be obnoxious and offensive to people. We don't have to wag our faith in other people's faces to be a faithful Kingdom citizen. But we do have to be willing to stand resolute and not waver when it comes to what we believe. It is one thing to live a faithful life and for everyone to know that you are a believer. It is another thing altogether to be shabby and snooty about it.

In order to effectively share our worldview with the community, it is necessary to faithfully live it out in life. This includes things like being honest, full of integrity, joyful, helpful, faithful, encouraging and all of the other things that are expressions of the Spirit of God living in our lives.

After sharing our worldview, *it is necessary to intentionally inject ourselves into various aspects of the community for the purpose of getting the Kingdom worldview out there*. The focus, here, is on purpose. It is not good enough just to join and be a part of various groups. The reason for joining has to be for the purpose of expressing your faith. As you become a productive and faithful member of a group, there will come times when you have a platform for expressing your worldview. And when that happens, some people will want to know even more. Look for every opportunity to bring people to the gates of the Kingdom. Whether or not they enter is their own decision. But your responsibility is to bring them to the gate.

Once we have become faithful in allowing the Kingdom to be actively expressed in our lives, we are then in a position to take on some of the specific evils that enter into the culture. We do have a responsibility to protect our culture. But it is not for the sake of protecting culture! It is for the sake of working together with God to accomplish his purposes by helping other individuals who might be harmed by the evil influences in the culture.

When sexual immorality, pornography, homosexuality, abortion, profanity, fraud, pedophilia, prostitution, cheating, racism, alcohol and drug abuse, smoking, gluttony, and so on become normalized in a culture, people who might have an inclination to be drawn into those things are put at risk. Children are particularly vulnerable to the influences of adults that they look up to when they see them participating in immoral behavior.

This is not to say that individuals who choose to walk the path of evil are, themselves, without blame. Ultimately every person has to accept full responsibility for the choices they make. But *normalizing evil in a society makes it easier for individuals to make wrong decisions.* It assures that there will be more people participating in evil activities which are creating problems within the culture.

The purpose of our activity in working against evil is not to save the culture, though that will be a beneficial byproduct. Our purpose is to save individuals from going down a path that will lead to their spiritual and eternal destruction. It is essential to keep the purpose out front. When you focus on the activity rather than the people, you end up with an "ends justifies the means" mentality. That is when you see people who are willing to murder doctors for performing abortions, and you witness hate-filled tirades against people of other religions.

We do need to work against the murder of the unborn, against the normalization of homosexuality and pornography, against more violence and sex on TV and the like. But it needs to be in the context of helping people come to a personal relationship with God through Jesus Christ, and not simply as a cause to help us feel we are doing something useful.

Take Care of the World

We certainly have a duty to be active in taking care of our own community, but our responsibility does not end there. God has also commanded us to participate in extending the reach of the Kingdom to other material cultures beyond our own. There are a couple of ways we can do this.

First, we can assist the expansion of the Kingdom by *financially supporting organizations and individuals who are actively engaging other cultures for that purpose.* Again, the ultimate purpose of the activity is not to change culture—it is to extend the reach of the Kingdom into the lives of people who do not have a relationship with God. As this happens, though, cultures will be affected.

The second thing we can do is to *personally support the worldwide expansion of the Kingdom by actually going to other cultures and doing Kingdom work.* In our day there are more ways to do this than ever before in the history of mankind. There are certainly opportunities to do it as a career, and there are many missionary sending organizations which facilitate people taking this career path. But that is not the life calling of most Kingdom citizens.

That being said, there are still opportunities for the rest of us. There are literally thousands of short-term projects that allow individuals to participate personally in the work of the Kingdom around the globe. In addition to that, the world is, literally, at our doorstep. Go to virtually any city, or even small towns around the country, and you will find pockets of people from other cultures.

Finally, it is also possible to support and participate with organizations which fight evil elements of culture that are widespread around the globe. Things such as slavery, child exploitation, the global sex trade, international dope peddling, and organized crime need to be confronted and eradicated.

It is our spiritual duty to work to *influence* cultures. That does not mean to Americanize them. Rather, to inject in them the qualities of the Kingdom of God.

A War Fought on Two Levels

People who think only of eternal issues can do a lot of good in the lives of those they influence. But they end up leaving a lot of loose ends as the forces of evil continue having sway over the ones they have influenced.

People who only work at the material level to try and rid the world of war, abortion, slavery, child exploitation, domestic violence, homelessness, gambling, murder, and the like, can also do a lot of good. But operating at that level alone results in passing over the thing that gives life its meaning.

The war against the forces of evil is fought on two levels—the spiritual and the material. Anyone who tries to leave one of them out is only doing first aid when what is really needed is a cure.

Digging Deeper

1. What are you doing personally to make yourself more effective in accomplishing the work of the Kingdom?
2. What are you doing personally to make your family more effective in accomplishing the work of the Kingdom?
3. What are you doing personally to make your community conform more to the Kingdom?
4. What are you doing personally to make the world conform more to the Kingdom?

As I look over my life, I must say I have mellowed a lot over the years. I used to be much more competitive than I am now. I would see something I wanted, confront it head on and do my best to win. I still have this drive to win, but my approach to winning is so different now.

First it is different regarding how I define "winning." Over the years I have come to realize that some things are more important than others. It is actually possible to win a battle but, in doing so, to lose the war.

Another thing that I have learned is that sometimes an indirect approach is much more effective than a direct approach. It is sort of like Judo where, instead of confronting an opponent directly, you use a person's weight and momentum against them and, basically, let them defeat themselves.

The issues that emerge as cultural conflicts are certainly important—important enough to fight for. But if you lose sight of the underlying foundation that makes the issue important, you may win the battle and lose the war.

Our focus, as Christians, has to be the big picture—the very purposes of God. He wants people living a moral life but not just for the sake of following a list of rules. He doesn't just want us to do holy things, he wants us to become holy people.

When I finally figured this out, my life changed. That was the point when everything began to make sense and my life began to take on purpose and meaning that I had never known before.

Chapter 16

The Battle Belongs to the Lord

This is love for God: to obey his commands. And his commands are not burdensome, for everyone born of God overcomes the world. This is the victory that has overcome the world, even our faith. 1 John 5:3-4

There is a battle tactic that has been used with great effectiveness over the years. It is kind of cruel to some of the warriors because it deliberately sacrifices some of the soldiers in order to get the win, but it is very effective, just the same. Here's how it works.

Two opposing armies are lined up in a field facing one another. Army number one puts its weakest soldiers in the middle of the line. As the armies charge each other, the weak soldiers in the middle begin getting killed and a hole is opened up in the middle of the battlefield where they were. Naturally, army number two moves more and more into the hole where there is less resistence. Then, suddenly, army number one has its soldiers, who are on the end, swing around the sides, and the second army finds itself quickly surrounded and unable to defend itself.

God is smart like that. He is in a battle against evil, and he knows how to win it. In the end, there is no doubt who will be the victor. God has already laid the traps, and he outflanks any who try to oppose him. But he doesn't do it as an act of cruelty. In fact, just the opposite.

The forces of evil are the agents of destruction. They destroy individuals, and they destroy societies. When evil is put aside, both individuals and societies know harmony and prosperity.

God created us to be in relationship with himself and to show our love to him. That is what we should be spending our time doing. Along with that he has called us to be involved in a particular mission. He wants us to work with him in helping influence others to make the choice to enter a relationship with himself. But God, and only God, has the power to change a person's heart, and he only uses that power when an individual makes the personal choice to follow him.

Every Kingdom citizen is called to live faithfully in relationship with God. Every Kingdom citizen is called to be an instrument of God and to share the advantages of Kingdom citizenship with those who are not yet citizens. Every Kingdom citizen has a calling to overlay Kingdom culture over all expressions of material culture, but it is left to God to add the final touch.

It is not our job to do everything, but it is our job to do what has been given to us individually. Do you know what your mission is? If you don't, you should not rest until you have discovered it. That is how important it is! It expresses the very reason for your existence. You will never find fulfillment in life until you are doing it. You will never fulfill your destiny until you are actively engaged in extending the Kingdom by means of the calling God has given to you.

Fulling your destiny will require tremendous courage. Every world-view has a vested interest in protecting itself. You will face opposition! Fighting the culture war is definitely not for wimps, but it is the calling of God for our lives.

It is time for you to get out there and engage the world according to your calling. It is your turn to fight the culture war in the way God has directed that it be fought. Take the time to confront people in the arena of worldview. Show them how they can know a personal relationship with God. Their lives, and yours, will be changed—and culture along with it.

Digging Deeper

1. What do you understand to be God's purpose for the world?
2. What, specifically, do you understand to be your part in fulfilling God's purpose?
3. What are you doing to fulfill that purpose?

Endnotes

Chapter 7
1 Matthew 7:24-27

Chapter 10
1 Genesis 1:1, Psalm 19:1, Hebrews 11:3
2 Genesis 1:1-2:25, Psalm 33:9
3 Isaiah 40:13-14, Daniel 4:35, Ephesians 1:11, Acts 1:7-8
4 Matthew 28:18-20, Luke 17:20-21
5 Job 42:2, Psalm 22:27-28, Revelation 19:6
6 John 14:23, 2 Corinthians 6:16-18
7 Genesis 1:27, Genesis 9:5-6
8 Luke 16:19-31
9 John 3:18
10 1 John 4:8
11 Psalm 99:9
12 Psalm 119: 137-138, Romans 10:3-4
13 Luke 17:20_21

Chapter 11
1 Romans 10:9-15
2 Philippians 2:5-11
3 1 Timothy 2:3-4
4 John 3:16-18
5 Genesis 2:15 - 3:13
6 Genesis 6:1-8
7 Judges 2:1-23
8 Luke 18:18-23
9 Matthew 9:9
10 Matthew 4:18-20
11 Luke 19:1-10
12 Romans 12:1-2, Hebrews 2:1-5, James 4:4-7, 1 Peter 4:1-6, 1 John 1:15-17
13 Hebrews 10:16, James 1:16-18, 2 Peter 1:3-4, 1 John 2:27

Chapter 12
1 Romans 3:23
2 Romans 6:23
3 John 3:16
4 Revelation 3:20
5 Ephesians 4:15-16, 1 Peter 2:2-3

Worldview and Culture Resources

This list is not intended to be an exhaustive roster of resources. It is simply a starting place for those who wish to investigate this topic further. The books and websites that are listed give references to other sources, as well. Please note that websites, in particular, are constantly changing. The ones listed are active as of this printing.

Additionally, there may be sources, links or articles in some of these sources that may be questionable. It is up to you to discern what is truth as you read.

Books

Barna, George. *Think Like Jesus.* Integrity Publishers, 2003.

Colson, Charles, Pearcey, Nancy. *How Now Shall We Live?* Tyndale House Publishers, 1999.

Moreland, J.P. *Love Your God With All Your Mind.* Navpress Publishing Group, 1997.

Pearcey, Nancy. *Total Truth* Crossway Books, 2004.

Shaeffer, Francis. *How Then Should We Live?* Fleming H Revell Co., 1976.

Shaeffer, Francis. *A Christian Manifesto.* Crossway Books, 1981.

Shaeffer, Francis. *He Is There and He Is Not Silent.* Tyndale House Publishers. 1972.

Sire, James. *Why Should Anyone Believe Anything at All?* Downers Grove: InterVarsity Press, 1994.

Sire, James. *The Universe Next Door.* 3rd ed., Downers Grove, IL: InterVarsity Press, 1997.

Sire, James. *Naming the Elephant: Worldview as a Concept*. Downers Grove: InterVarsity Press, 2004.

Stroble, Lee. *The Case for a Creator*. Zondervan, 2004.

Helpful Websites

Probe Ministries - http://www.probe.org

RZIM - http://www.rzim.org

Institute of Biblical Defense - http://www.biblicaldefense.org

BreakPoint - http://www.pfm.org/BPTemplate.cfm

Focus on the Family - http://www.family.org

Crosswalk.com - http://www.crosswalk.com

Soulation - http://soulation.org/

The Christian Worldview Webpage - http://members.aol.com/theotrek/index.html?f=fs

Ministryandmedia.com - http://www.ministryandmedia.com

Josh McDowell Ministry - http://www.josh.org

Biblical Worldview - http://www.christianworldview.net

Worldview Academy - http://www.worldview.org

Stand to Reason - http://www.str.org
Nehemiah Institute - http://www.nehemiahinstitute.com

Leadership U - http://www.leaderu.com/

The Seven Worldview Questions

1. What is the most fundamental reality? (Ultimate reality)
2. What is the nature of our material reality? (Material reality)
3. What is a human being? (Humanity)
4. What happens to a person at death? (Death)
5. Why is it possible to know anything at all? (Knowledge)
6. How do we know what is right and wrong? (Morality)
7. What is the meaning of human history? (History)

Taken from Dr. James Sire's book, *The Universe Next Door*, 3rd ed., Downers Grove, IL: InterVarsity Press, 1997, pp. 17-18.

Summary Explanation of the
Basic Worldviews

Naturalism

Naturalism assumes that there is no "built-in" meaning or purpose for anything. Human life, indeed every kind of life, and every aspect of material reality are just enormous cosmic accidents. The essence of reality is nothing more than material substances which, over the eons, have evolved to what we see today.

Since there is no ultimate moral purpose or meaning in anything, it is simply up to the creatures who are capable of contemplation to invent their own meaning. To this point in evolutionary history, only man has ended up evolving with a sense of moral values or purpose, so only man needs to deal with this issue. Ultimately, since there is no innate value or meaning, each person has to find their own meaning—something subjective that makes life meaningful and worth living for them. It may be different from individual to individual but that is OK. There is nothing that can objectively be called right, truth, purpose, or meaning.

Animism

Animism assumes that any kind of unexplained event happens because spiritual beings or supernatural forces are at work in the natural world. Certainly natural forces are recognized as operating in situations where a natural cause can be readily seen. But in cases where a natural cause cannot be seen, it is automatically assumed to be caused by supernatural power.

Far Eastern Thought

The ultimate end of the most prominent forms of Far Eastern Thought is absorption into an all-encompassing cosmos. No one is able to take seriously any kind of objective reality—whether knowledge or sensory experience. It is acknowledged that there is such a thing as objective reality, but it goes on to assert that the nature of that reality is quite beyond our ability to comprehend. The goal of life, therefore, is to simply recognize that reality cannot be known and to passively live life. This attitude frees a person from all of the suffering that "seems" to be all around. When the state of total passivity is achieved, individuals are freed to simply let life come as it will.

Theism

Theism, in a general sense, gives us all the categories necessary to get a handle on truth by providing a framework for understanding both the material and the spiritual aspects of existence. It points to God as creator, gives a basis for natural and spiritual law, and holds out the hope that there is a reason and purpose for our existence.

The big problem with theism, as a category, is that it is so broad. It encompasses several of the major world religions as well as dozens of smaller groups. Many, if not most, of these groups have their own authoritative book which they consider to be an actual revelation from God. Most do not, however, contemplate a God who is interested in intimate interaction with the material world and man, in particular.

Various theistic approaches go in very different directions, some of which contradict one other. This means that not every specific theistic view can be viable. Theism does generally, point us in the right direction, but we need to find the specific view of theism that we can acknowledge as truth.

Relational Revelation

Relational Revelation is a specialized form of Theism and is the only worldview that allows for a completely coherent and comprehensive understanding of our perceptions of reality, and which has a basis for backing it up. This does not mean that we will get answers to every question that we want answered. There are certainly some things that we long to know which are beyond our human ability to understand.

The pure view, though, does cover all of the bases. There are categories for understanding the part of reality that we interact with physically and for understanding that part which is beyond the reach of the senses. And it does all of this in a way that matches up with the way human beings actually experience life.

Basic Values Promoted by Each Worldview

Naturalism

When a group forms, they decide, based on their own perceived needs, what kind of values and behaviors will be useful for the survival of the group. If the condition or situation changes, there is no compelling reason why the cultural elements can't also be changed. Morality is simply what the group wants it to be.

Animism

The world and life are not moving toward a higher destination so the tendency is simply to live life one day at a time and accept things the way they are. Left to themselves, animistic cultures tend to remain living in primitive circumstances with very little societal advancement.

Eastern Pantheistic Monism

The primary impact of Far Eastern Religion on culture is to promote passivism.

Theism

Theism basically lends itself to an impact on culture that is both moral and positive, but most forms result in a legalistic approach to living life and the development of culture. The moral order ought to be a certain way because it is written in the law or put forth by the prophet. The way things ought to be are specifically prescribed.

Relational Revelation

Relational Revelation lends itself to an impact on culture that is both moral and positive. It does all of this in a way that puts a priority on a personal relationship with God as the motivation for fulfilling the purposes of God. It is not just the end result that matters. The means by which the outcome is brought about is also vital. The means are conveyed by personal instruction from God to individual human beings.

About the Author

Dr. Freddy Davis is involved in a wide variety of ministry activities. His is currently a seminar speaker, Executive Director of MarketFaith Ministries, church staff member and the owner of TSM Enterprises. He received his BS in Communications from Florida State University as well as an MDiv and DMin from Southwestern Baptist Theological Seminary. He spent 16 years overseas serving as a missionary (11 years in Japan and 5 years in the former Soviet Republic of Latvia).

As a conference speaker, Freddy speaks to businesses and other organizations on the topics of personal development, decision making, influence, customer service and leadership.

He is also available to churches and other Christian organizations to speak on the topics of prayer, understanding the culture war and how worldview affects your ability to faithfully live the Christian life. Freddy lives in Tallahassee, Florida, with his wife, Deborah and son, Ken.

For more information...
On speaking engagements or other resources from Dr. Freddy Davis,
Contact him by e-mail: davis@iname.com
Or fax him at 850-514-4571.
Also, visit his website at http://www.marketfaith.org and
http://www.tsmenterprises.com